Editor's Note

Beijing is the capital of the People's Republic of China. Over 860 years ago, Jin Dynasty (1115–1234) emperor Wanyan Liang (reign: 1149–1161) chose it as the location of the capital and named it Zhongdu, marking the beginning of Beijing's history as a capital.

Beijing has changed greatly in more than 860 years, but, even as it becomes a World City with Chinese characteristics, it still retains some of the features of the layout established when it first became a capital city.

Throughout its history, Beijing has been renowned for its design. In the Yuan Dynasty (1271–1368), the Central Axis became an urban planning masterpiece and the city became world-famous, and has since attracted visitors from home and abroad. Ancient structures are now complemented by new landmarks.

Beijing also has rich culture that can share with the whole world. More than 860 years ago, Song Dynasty (AD 960–1279) philosopher Zhang Zai's concepts of inclusiveness, people-orientation, exploration and peace took root and gradually grew throughout the city, contributing to the development of Beijing's civilisation.

Beijing is also known for its art. During the Yuan Dynasty and throughout the city's history, Chinese people's pursuit of beauty was reflected in every corner of Beijing and numerous artistic and cultural masterpieces were created.

As a capital for more than 860 years, Beijing has cultivated countless talents. Its history reflected its tremendous changes, nourished its profound culture and witnessed its great efforts to establish traditions and make innovations for a better future.

Beijingers are proud of the city's history as a capital, a history worth exploring and cherishing. This issue highlights some of the most fascinating aspects of that history.

This is Beijing!

Magic Square, Capital of All Cities

With the camera ascending, he gradually sat up, his eyes fixed on the monitor. This was a wonderful moment, as the charm of the city gradually spread out below him. Although he had been to this Asian capital many times, Bernardo Bertolucci never had such a panoramic view of the imperial city. "This city is like a magic square," he said, expressing how the breathtaking, magnificent style of Beijing impressed him.

Many years later, in 2011, Bertolucci, an Italian, appeared in a wheelchair at the Cannes Film Festival to receive a Lifetime Achievement Award. On August 16, 1986, he began making *The Last Emperor*, "… the most time-consuming and demanding film," in Beijing. The film won a number of awards and he became the first foreign director permitted to film inside the Forbidden City.

He repeated the same message to foreigners who had not had the chance to visit Beijing during the early years of China's Reform and Opening. "Beijing is a magic square."

That is an appropriate simile. Beijing actually originated from a square fortress. Over 860 years, it has been built, rebuilt, enlarged and renovated, just like a magic square with multiple parts fitted together.

Contents

Magic Square, Capital of All Cities	2
Seat of Supreme Power, City of Emperors	9
Rich Soil, the Land Where Dragons Hide	20
Finding Life in Opera	29
Painting, Dance of Colours	39
Poetry as a Recorder of History	50
Legendary Chinese Costume	61

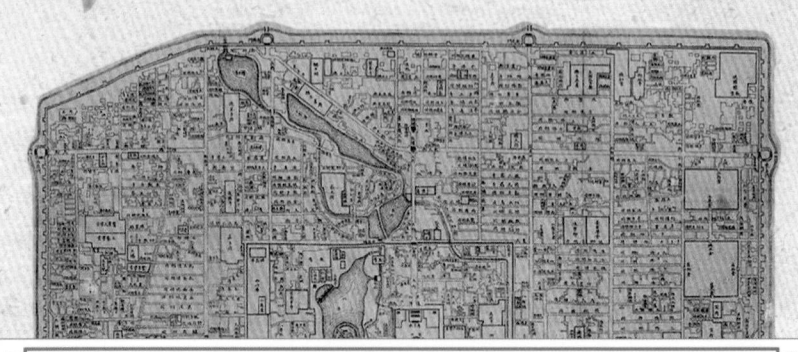

BEIJING'S HISTORICAL STORIES

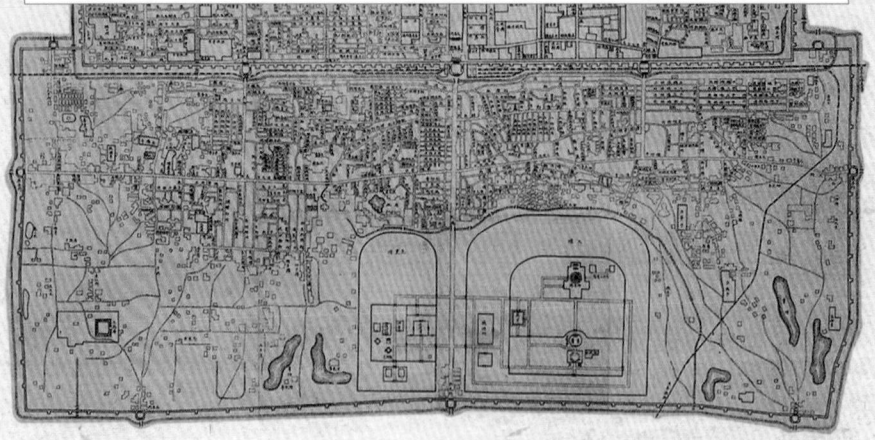

An Expedition across Changbai Mountain and Heilongjiang River

Two inspiring archaeological discoveries have shed light on the history of Beijing as a capital.

The first discovery was in October 1990, at a dormitory construction site in Yulin Block, You'anmenwai, by the Beijing Municipal Bureau of Forestry and Parks: the site of a water gate at the south wall of Zhongdu, or Central Capital, of the Jin Dynasty. It was rated among the top ten archaeological discoveries that year. The People's Government of Beijing Municipality immediately decided to build the Museum of Liao and Jin City Walls on the site. Water gates were openings beneath the city wall that allowed rivers to flow in and out of the old city. The Jin water gate was made of logs and stones. The superstructure is missing but the base remains, making it the largest water gate of its kind discovered in China. It also helps identify the exact location of Zhongdu's southern wall.

The second discovery was on June 3, 2010, a significant day for Beijing. In the Lize Financial Business District, which was under construction at the time, a 1,000-square-metre site dating to Zhongdu was found in northern Fenghuangzui Village in Fengtai District. The Jin Zhongdu City Wall Relic Park is located 21 metres to its south. Many relics were excavated from the site, and have proved valuable in understanding the history of Beijing as a capital.

In addition to the above two major excavations, 20 years apart, many finds have been made across the city that have helped to reveal the site of Zhongdu.

In 2003, a monument was set up on the site of Zhongdu's Da'an Palace, identifying April 21, 1153, as the day Beijing officially became a capital for the first time. On that day, 850 years before the monument was unveiled, Wanyan Liang, the fourth emperor (reign: 1150–61) of the Jin Dynasty, ordered his subjects from Northeast China to settle in the new capital.

Wanyan Liang, sometimes referred to as Emperor Hailingwang of Jin, after seizing the throne by murdering his predecessor, deliberated on how he could consolidate his position. He decided to build a new capital in Beijing. He was deeply influenced by the Chinese culture and thus eager for ethnic unity. Cruel but ambitious, he built the new capital as an inclusive, fashionable and elegant city. According to accounts in *Jin Shi (The History of the Jin Dynasty)*, huge amounts of manpower and resources were devoted to the construction. "Twenty million silver pieces was spent to transport a log and 500 labourers dragged a cart." We can only imagine how luxurious this imperial city was through these accounts.

However, Beijing served as the capital of the Jin Dynasty for only 61 years. The city later belonged to several successive dynasties and experienced many ups and downs, peace and war. Inevitably, much has been lost.

In 2001, the Museum of Liao and Jin City Walls conducted a survey of relics from the Liao (AD 916–1125) and Jin dynasties in all of Beijing's districts and counties. It identified 15 Liao pagodas, nine Jin pagodas and Lugou Bridge (Marco Polo Bridge) as the extant aboveground buildings from the two dynasties. In addition, there are 19 tombs, more than 30 Buddhist cellars, more than 30 sites and relics, 18 stone tablets, five Buddhist stone caskets and 11 gravestones.

Considering the cultural splendour of Beijing as an imperial capital, there should be more relics from the two dynasties. Emperor Wanyan Liang made his permanent mark through his various gardens, such as Beihai Park, the Fragrant Hills, Diaoyutai, Yuquan Hill, Taoran Pavilion and Yuyuantan, which he visited at intervals between wars. What we now know as "the Eight Scenes of Yanjing," originated during the Jin Dynasty.

Capital of a Prosperous Dynasty

"Streets in Dadu are all designed in straight lines, running from wall to wall. If you stand on a city gate, you can see the gate on the opposite side of the city. There are various shops and stalls on both sides of streets. The whole city is a square, like a chessboard." There are many accounts of Dadu such as this in *The Travels of Marco Polo.* If he were to introduce the same city to the world today, the legendary Italian explorer would probably also describe it as a magic square, since the ancient city in his book was the origin of his compatriot Bertolucci's magic square.

According to various historical accounts and paintings, the Yuan Dynasty's (1271–1368) Dadu was a "globalised metropolis," and its openness was unparalleled among contemporary cities. Merchants, warriors, adventurers, travellers, diplomats, missionaries and artists from all over the world came to the city to live, work, trade and enjoy doing whatever they liked to their hearts' content. According to *The Travels of Marco Polo,* "Big hotels and taverns were built about one mile away from the city walls in the suburbs to provide accommodation to travellers and merchant groups. There are designated places for people from different countries. For example, one place is for Lombards, one for Germans and one for French. Whenever envoys or ambassadors come to Dadu for dealings with the Great Khan, they are accommodated and entertained by the imperial court."

The history of the Yuan Dynasty has long fascinated historians because of the merging of ethnic groups and civilisations. They believe Dadu was more than the capital of Yuan emperors, who ruled vast territories. It was the capital of all cities. Genghis Khan and his descendants conquered a vast stretch of land from China in the east to the Danube in the west. They swept aside borders and barriers, securing traffic and trade between the East and the West. Several ancient civilisations were brought into contact with each other. Dadu, as the capital of an empire, was inclusive, incorporating various cultures into its own.

Marco Polo must have had a profound love for Dadu. In his book, he described the imperial city, palaces, squares, streets, city walls and gates. Thanks to his accounts, we can now appreciate the grandeur of a great empire. "Dadu is square in shape, with a circumference of 24 miles. The city is surrounded by a trapezium wall that measures 10 steps at the base and only three steps at the top. The battlements are white. Streets in Dadu are all designed in straight lines, running from wall to wall. If you stand on a city gate, you can see the gate on the opposite side of the city. There are various shops and stalls on both sides of streets. All yards in the city are square in shape and are aligned in straight lines. In each yard, there is enough space for buildings and gardens." What a wonderful utopia it is!

It is rather a pity that such a prosperous capital described by numerous travellers from around the world can only be "excavated" by archaeologists today. The Park of Yuan Dadu Relics, which was excavated and built from 1957 to 2006, is the only place where people in Beijing can find traces of this once powerful empire. In 1271, Kublai Khan named his empire the Yuan, which means "origin," according to the *Yijing (The Book of Changes)*. He changed the name of the city from Yanjing to Dadu and established it as the capital. The Yuan Dynasty's territory once stretched to the Arctic Ocean to the north, the Sea of Japan to the east, the Pamir Mountains to the west and Vietnam to the south. Its vastness was unprecedented and unparalleled in history. Today, the belt-shaped park stands on the site of the former Dadu to tell stories of Genghis Khan and his descendants.

Grandeur of the Forbidden City

"Beijing is unique in the world for its evenly proportioned design. Having been used to its chessboard layout, I often lose my way while in other provinces. The Forbidden City is the centre of the whole city, with its nine gates arranged in symmetry. Tiananmen is at the front while Di'anmen Gate is at the back. Dongbianmen Gate and Xibianmen Gate are at two corners, like the places for corner-kicks on a football pitch. The Drum and Bell Towers are in the north while the Temple of Heaven, the Altar of the Earth, the Altar of the Sun and the Altar of the Moon are on all four sides. Streets are named according to their location, such as Dongdan (East Single Archway), Xidan (West Single Archway), Nanchizi (South Moat) and Beichizi (North Moat)…" That is the description of Beijing in *Beijingcheng Zaji (Reminiscences of Beijing)* by Xiao Qian, a writer who worked as a war correspondent in Britain during World War II. The "square city" he described is Beijing, the complex magic square that dates back to the Ming (1368–1644) and Qing (1644–1911) dynasties.

The last emperor of the Yuan Dynasty (1271–1368) surrendered his capital to Ming Dynasty general Xu Da and fled the city. He went back to the Mongolian grassland to live as his ancestors: as a nomad. Xu Da, after taking the city, was ordered to build a mansion for Zhu Di, the fourth son of Zhu Yuanzhang (Emperor Hongwu; reign: 1368–98). In the first lunar month of 1403, Li Zhigang, then minister for ritual affairs, submitted a paper to Zhu Di (Emperor Yongle; reign: 1402–1424). It read, "Emperors in history all have a place of origin that bodes well for their empire. Beijing is the origin of your majesty, so it is appropriate to build it as the new capital." Li listed a number of historical facts to persuade Emperor Yongle. According to *Lüshi Chunqiu (Lü's Spring and Autumn),* "Emperors establish their capital in the middle of the country and build their palace in the middle of the capital." According to the *"Cheng Ma"* (an article) in the *Guanzi,* "A capital should be built at the foot of a mountain or on a vast plain. It should have a stable water source while being safe from floods." Beijing is located at the foot of Taihang Mountain and laced by rivers, with Mongolian deserts and grasslands to the north and Central China to the south. The prosperity of Dadu was still visible to Emperor Yongle, who knew that he must secure his hold on North China. Finally, in 1421, he officially named the city Beijing and established it as the capital of the Ming Dynasty. Aside from a few historical moments, Beijing has served as the capital ever since.

There are numerous architectural wonders from the Ming and Qing dynasties. Two architects, Kuai Xiang and Yang Shilei, together with their teams, designed and oversaw the construction of more than half of the classic buildings in Beijing.

According to various historical accounts, Kuai Xiang was the most prominent architect of the Ming Dynasty and the designer of Tian'anmen. In 1417, he went to Beijing and began his work on the imperial palace. The first task was to design and build the front gate, Chengtianmen (today's Tian'anmen). He finished the job on time, much to the emperor's satisfaction. He was then promoted to chief architect. Over the next 40 years, he designed the three grand palaces in the Forbidden City.

Unfortunately, all three were destroyed by fire in 1457. Eight years later, Emperor Yingzong (reign: 1436–49, 1457–64) asked him to build the wooden gate towers, palaces and official buildings. In 1464, he was put in charge of the construction of the Yu Tomb, one of the Ming Shisanling (the 13 Tombs of 13 Ming Dynasty emperors). After Chengtianmen was destroyed by fire, he built a new gate measuring 120 metres long and 33.7 metres high in 1464, which is today's Tian'anmen, having been renamed in 1651. Because of his work, Kuai Xiang was promoted from a mere workman to a deputy minister of construction. According to Ming history, he was the first to apply Suzhou paintings and gilded bricks in architecture. He is, in fact, the founding father of Beijing we know today.

In early 2012, 54-year-old fitness teacher Lei Zhangbao, a descendant of Designer Lei, was interviewed by *Beijing* magazine. Without being explicit, he showed his respect for his ancestors and his hope for carrying forward their legacy. For most people unfamiliar with the history of architecture in Beijing, Designer Lei is little known. In *Zhongguo Jianzhu yu Zhongguo Jianzhushi (Chinese Architecture and Chinese Architects),* Liang Sicheng wrote, "In the Qing Dynasty, architects for the Imperial City of Beijing became hereditary positions. The family who won the position was called Designer Lei." In September 2012, Designer Lei was included as the fifth "World Memory Heritage" from China. Now, there are blueprints and models on display in the Forbidden City. The Yuanmingyuan (Old Summer Palace), Forbidden City, Temple of Heaven, Summer Palace, East Qing Tombs, West Qing Tombs and the Chengde

Mountain Resort, which have all been listed as World Heritage sites, were designed by the Lei family. The 83 models on display in the Forbidden City were used when rebuilding the Old Summer Palace, the Summer Palace and the West Garden during the reigns of Emperors Tongzhi (1861–75) and Guangxu (1875–1908). Today, blueprints belonging to Designer are likely the only records left detailing ancient Chinese architecture. The Lei family, who were masters of feng shui and design, established the grand and delicate style of the imperial buildings in Beijing. Their architectural designs aligned manmade structures with the natural terrain and Beijing's environment, achieving harmony between man and nature.

Architecture is a reflection of history and culture. Since the founding of the People's Republic of China in 1949, Beijing has witnessed rapid changes. New landmarks have repeatedly emerged to mark the skyline of the city, combining the ancient with the modern. The ancient sites and relics are evidence of the city's splendid past, the basis for its bright future.

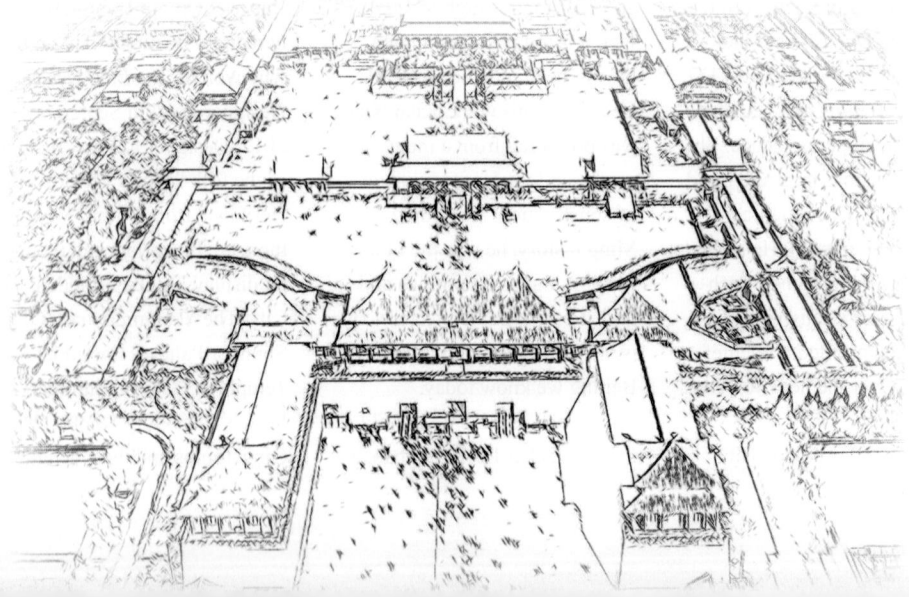

Seat of Supreme Power, City of Emperors

It is a popular toy all over the world, a set of plastic bricks that can be snapped together to build all kinds of structures. It is called Lego and was created in Denmark in 1932. As a big Lego fan, Baobao, a six-year-old girl who adores her collection of Lego classic architecture models, including the Guggenheim Museum, decided to write a letter to Lego headquarters. She hoped Lego would consider making an "architecture of Beijing" series, as there is a wealth of ancient structures in Beijing, which has been home to a total of 42 emperors who ruled the country during Beijing's 860-year history as the national capital.

The Chinese called the emperor's throne "the dragon throne." From the time the Jin Dynasty (1115–1234) moved its capital to Beijing in 1153 to the abdication of China's last emperor in 1912, Beijing has been the seat of power for 42 emperors, who descended from four ethnic groups: Nuchen, Mongolian, Han and Manchu. They ruled their subjects from the city, fostering the economy and culture and turning Beijing into an inclusive city that blended the cultures of China's various nationalities.

A Warm Land Suitable for Lotus Flower

A city, like a person, has its own destiny and the origins of Beijing as the capital can be connected to a great figure in history.

In 1149, Wanyan Liang (reign: 1149–61), then 28 and a grandson of former Emperor Taizu of the Jin Dynasty, assassinated Emperor Xizong (reign: 1135–49) and became the new emperor, beginning his 12-year rule. He is said to have been a merciless killer and a tyrant. It is recorded that he killed as many as 300 people on his way to seizing the throne. Unsure of his authority after the coup, he was uneasy in Huining Mansion, Shangjing (today's Acheng in Heilongjiang Province), which had been the Jin capital for 34 years, so he decided to move to Beijing, which gave rise to a popular story: During a dinner, he said to one of his ministers, "I planted two hundred lotuses, but they all died. Why?" The minister answered, "Citrus grows well only in the south of Yangtze River. That is due to the climate. Shangjing is too cold for lotus, but Beijing is warm enough." Then Wanyan Liang said, "Good, so we shall move the capital to Beijing."

In *Jin Shi (The History of Jin),* Wanyan Liang is described as an aspiring statesman who understood Chinese culture. Therefore, his decision to move the capital must have been a considered one rather than a careless whim. At the time, Shangjing was a remote place and shipping to the capital was extremely difficult and costly. And it was difficult to rule the whole country from a capital located in the far north of the vast empire. "The empire covered a land of thousands of miles. The North was sparsely populated and administration was simple, while the South was densely populated and administration was complex." It was expensive, both in time and money, to transport grain and cloth from the south to Shangjing. In addition, the palaces in Yanjing (as Beijing was then known), the capital of the Liao empire conquered by the Jin, remained in good shape, so it was suitable as the new capital in terms of geopolitics, economy and administration.

The year 1153 marked a watershed in the history of Beijing, as the first emperor established his new capital there and named it Zhongdu (central capital) of Jin.

Seven emperors in the Jin Dynasty, from Wanyan Liang to Wanyan Chenglin, who died the day after his coronation in 1234, ruled from Beijing. Whatever the criticisms of Wanyan Liang, he made a great contribution to the construction of Beijing. Zhongdu was a masterpiece at the time. Designers and constructors included Han people, Bohai people and people from other ethnic groups who lived in Yanjing. They infused their own cultures into the architecture. Wanyan Liang was a great admirer of Han culture, so the general design of the palaces followed that of Bianjing, the capital of the Northern Song Dynasty (AD 960–1127). Before construction started, Wanyan Liang asked painters to draw detailed layouts of the palaces of Bianjing and ordered Minister Zhang Haobei to build according to these pictures. Therefore, the layout and even many of the names of palaces in Zhongdu were the same as or similar to those of Bianjing. Wanyan Liang also had some parts of the palaces in Bianjing used in the construction. Some of the furniture and furnishings were taken from Bianjing and used in palaces of Zhongdu. Over the following 60 years of construction and renovation, Zhongdu's grandeur was unprecedented.

Wanyan Liang was also a talented poet, the best among Jin emperors, who were all accomplished literati. His writing was as grand in style as his aspirations to unify the country. One of his poems contains the lines, "Everything has been unified in the country. How can there be an independent state south of the Yangtze River? A million troops will soon conquer the West Lake, And I will ride a horse up to the highest mountain in Wu!" Although there are few Jin relics in Beijing now, Wanyan Liang ushered in a new era for the city.

City of Gold Could not Contain the Soul of Conquerors

"Wherever he was, the Great Khan must follow certain conventions. His table was higher than that of others and he sat at the northern end of the hall. He faced south, with his empress sitting on the left and his sons and nephews sitting on the right, while other members of the imperial family sat around at low places, with their heads at the same height as the feet of the Great Khan. Wives sat at the low tables on the right of the Great Khan according to their positions. Everyone sat at their designated place so that the Khan could see all of them." The man who wrote the above account claimed he had been granted an audience by Emperor Kublai Khan and had been his favourite guest in Dadu (Beijing). That man was Marco Polo, an Italian in his early twenties when he arrived in Dadu. He toured the country before going back to his homeland and writing *The Travels of Marco Polo*, a popular book, though one which has been challenged by many critics. It was from his book that Westerners came to know of the mysterious East and Kublai Khan, the "Caesar of China."

In Yuan Dadu Relic Park, there is a magnificent sculpture of Kublai Khan, who seems to be enjoying a commanding view of his empire's capital. His empire was unprecedented in terms of size and his warriors had conquered places that extended the empire's boundaries to limits never dreamed of before. According to historical records, the conquests of the Yuan Dynasty "began from the Gobi Desert and included the west of China, West Xia, Nuchen, Korea, Nanzhao and south of the Yangtze River. Finally, the country was unified and the territory extended across Yin Shan to the north, to the desert in the west, across the Liao River in the east and to the coast in the south. The territory of the Han Dynasty (206 BC–AD 220) extended 4,600 kilometres from east to west and 6,700 kilometres from north to south, and the territory of the Tang Dynasty (AD 618–907) extended 4,700 kilometres from east to west and 8,500 kilometres from north to south. The territory of the Yuan extended to the same extreme in the southeast as Han and Tang, while in the northwest, it extended far beyond the previous boundaries."

In 1206, Genghis Khan established the Great Mongol Empire. By November 1271, his grandson Kublai Khan had stabilised his rule, so he changed the name of the empire to "the Great Yuan", which comes from *Yi Jing (I Ching)*. The empire did not only belong to the Mongols. Rather, it was the continuation of dynasties in China. In February 1272, Kublai Khan changed Beijing's then name of Zhongdu to Dadu on the advice of his favourite minister, Liu Bingzhong. He established his capital here and, in 1273, his new palaces were completed. In the first month of the following year, Kublai sat in the Grand Palace of the Imperial City to accept the celebration of ministers. Eleven of the 15 khans of the Yuan Dynasty, from Kublai Khan to Emperor Shundi, ruled from Beijing and presided over another era of ethnic assimilation, as well as political, economic and cultural prosperity.

In *Weida de Zhongzhouxian (The Great Central Axis)*, architect Liang Sicheng wrote of "the longest and greatest central axis, which runs eight kilometres from north to south through the city. The unique grand order of Beijing originates from the axis. That general layout on such a grand scale is unparalleled in the world." The central axis in Beijing originated from Jin Dynasty on a small scale. However, the large axis, as described by Liang Sicheng, began with Dadu during the reign of Kublai Khan. In the history of the architecture of Beijing, Kublai Khan is a key figure.

During his 35-year-reign, Kublai Khan built Dadu into a truly international metropolis. The architecture of the buildings in the city was a mixture of different cultures. The ruler Kublai Khan was Mongol, the chief designer Liu Bingzhong was Han, the chief engineer was from Arabia, and many residents were Arabs, who brought with them the architectural styles of West Asia. In terms of urban economy, trade and commerce, Dadu was a thriving metropolis. According to the account by Marco Polo, "In every suburb, hotels and taverns were built about one mile from the city wall. Merchants from different places, such as Lombardy, Germany and France, were designated different places. Merchants who served the Great Khan would be treated and entertained by the government." It can be understood from this account that there were frequent diplomatic and commercial exchanges between Dadu and countries in Europe and Asia. According to Marco Polo, Dadu was the logistical centre of the world. Anything precious and valuable in the world, such as jewels, pearls, drugs and spices from India, and goods from across the Empire, were exchanged in the city. Silks and satins from the southern provinces were sold in shops in the city. The interaction and exchange of culture and people came to a climax in Dadu during the reign of Kublai Khan.

Like other emperors in history, Kublai Khan was a patron of Han culture and elites, though he did not speak Chinese. He had many Han ministers and he followed the Han style of administration. He also fostered the creation of a new Mongolian script, which enabled translation and exchange between Mongolians and Han Chinese, thus facilitating the integration of different ethnic groups in China.

Monarchs are not immortals. Though the ruler of a great empire, Kublai Khan's later years were marred by misfortune, such as the death of his favourite empress, Chabi, and his heir apparent, Zhenjin, as well as setbacks in his expeditions in Japan and South Asia. When he was approaching 80, he led an army to defend Helin against another Mongol ruler. The battle proved too great a strain and he died before his 81st birthday.

In 1238, when Kublai Khan ordered the execution of Wen Tianxiang, the captured former prime minister of the Southern Song Dynasty (1127–1279), at Caishikou (today's Jiaodaokou), he ordered the removal of straw from walls and roofs for fear Dadu residents would set the city aflame. However, in the final days of the last Yuan ruler, Emperor Shundi, an army led by Zhu Yuanzhang did just that, reducing the city to ashes. The once gold city disappeared and the soul of Kublai Khan had to return to his Mongolian homeland.

Popular Heroes Deified

An inferno ended the rule of the Yuan Dynasty in Beijing. The strong northbound troops of Xu Da and Chang Yuchun paved the way for the founding of the Ming Dynasty. In early 1368, Emperor Taizu Zhu Yuanzhang, a man of humble origins, ascended the throne in Yingtian (today's Nanjing) and established the Ming Dynasty (1368–1644). As the dynasty between Yuan and Qing, Ming was a rejuvenation of Han, ending the rule of the Mongolians in China, but was also the last dynasty established by Han Chinese.

Of the 16 Ming emperors, from Emperor Chengzu (Emperor Yongle) Zhu Di, who moved the capital to Beijing, to Emperor Sizong Chongzhen, who hanged himself on Jingshan Hill, 14 ruled in Beijing. The history of Ming was a long one, flourishing at first, before falling into gradual decline, and was closely connected with the history of Beijing. Most of the landmarks in today's Beijing, such as the Forbidden City, the Temple of Heaven), the Imperial Ancestral Temple and the Temple of Ancient Monarchs, originated from the Ming Dynasty. Beijing became the place symbolising the authority of Ming emperors, leaving valuable architectural, historical and cultural legacies.

When Zhu Di ascended the throne as Emperor Yongle in 1402, he changed the name of Beiping to Beijing and began the construction of the imperial palace which lasted 18 years. At the same time, he renovated Huitong River and other sections of the Grand Canal in order to facilitate the smooth transport of grain and goods from the South to the North. In 1421, Zhu Di sat in Fengtian Palace in Beijing to give audience to his ministers and prayed at the

Temple of Heaven. This marked the completion of the capital's establishment in Beijing.

In his book *Zuguo Dahanghaijia Zheng He Zhuan (The Great Sailor Zheng He)*, Liang Qichao praised Zhu Di highly, "Emperor Chengzu was very strategic. After establishing his rule, he thought of projecting his power out of the country, just like Emperor Xiaowu of Han Dynasty (206 BC–220 AD) and Emperor Taizong of Tang Dynasty (AD 618–907) did. Emperor Chengzu repelled Mongols and conquered peripheral regions of his empire, so land transportation became very prosperous, as during the Han and Tang Dynasties. Then he thought of the voyages led by Zheng He." Emperor Chengzu ruled during the hight of the Ming Dynasty. He left two legacies of which the Chinese are still proud of. First, he ordered the compilation of *Yongle Dadian (The Yongle Canon)* by Xie Jin, Yao Guangxiao, Wang Jing and Zou Ji. It was the first and largest encyclopaedia in ancient China and the world, written 300 years earlier than *Encyclopaedia Britannica* and *The French Encyclopaedia,* which were both first published in the 18th century. Secondly, he ordered the construction of the Forbidden City. The plan was made in 1407 and the construction lasted from 1417 to 1420. The whole project was supervised by Chen Gui, with the designer Wu Zhong in charge. From 1407 onwards, Emperor Chengzu summoned architects and craftsmen from all over the country as well as 200,000–300,000 labourers to build the Forbidden City over 14 years. As one of the most famous structures in the world, the Forbidden City still retains its flavour of the Ming Dynasty today.

The building of ancestral shrines and temples was the wish of all emperors. Today, there is a popular saying in Beijing: "There is a bridge without water, a tablet without a base, a bell without a drum and a temple without Buddha." This is the Temple of Ancient Monarchs, located on the north side of Fuchengmennei Street in Xicheng District, built in 1530 during the reign of Emperor Jiajing (reign: 1522–66). It is the only extant imperial temple worshipping emperors of all dynasties. It had the same status as the Imperial Ancestral Temple and the Confucius Temple, being one of the three temples that the emperor himself worshipped at. According to the will of Emperor Jiajing, all emperors since the legendary–Three Sovereigns and Five Emperors of ancient China, together with major ministers who made important contributions, were worshipped here. Over the 380 years from its completion to the end of the Qing Dynasty, at least 662 ceremonies of worship were held there.

Emperors in China were not deities. Whatever ethnic group they came from and whatever aspirations they had, they were all elites of the Chinese people and were diligent in their administration, so they deserved the respect and commemoration of posterities. As a result, emperors and ministers worshipped in the temple came to be a deified group in China.

Ming Emperors include Zhu Yuanzhang, who had a humble origin as a beggar, Zhu Di, whose achievements are legendary but is regarded by posterity as merciless, Jiajing, who built the Temple of Ancient Monarchs but was engrossed in religious and superstitious activities and Chongzhen (reign: 1627–44), the last Ming emperor.

When it comes to Emperor Chongzhen, people in Beijing will always mention the tree in Jingshan Park, though the actual place of his suicide is still disputed today. As the last emperor, he ascended the throne when the dynasty was already in decline. In terms of apologising to the country, Emperor Chongzhen was a pioneer. He issued six decrees of apology during his reign, as peasant uprisings were widespread and the Qing army was threatening the peace on the borders. Natural catastrophes also threatened the nation. In 1644, the 35-year-old emperor issued his last decree of apology. As the uprising army led by Li Zicheng was besieging the city, the emperor had his last family dinner before arranging for the escape of his heir apparent Cilang, his third son Cijiong and fourth son Cihuan. Later, he killed his concubines and daughters while his empress hanged herself in Kunning Palace. On the next morning, he left the Forbidden City with his chief eunuch Wang Cheng'en and climbed up the imperial garden Mei Shan (today's Jing Shan in Jingshan Park) and wrote the following words, "Over 17 years of my reign, I have been ill-advised by my ministers, and the country is in turmoil. I am too ashamed to see my ancestors, so I take off my hat and cover my face with my hair. Let the uprising troops part my body, so that they will not kill my subjects." He then hanged himself on an old scholar tree, bringing to end the rule of the Ming Dynasty.

The Long Gone Palaces

A central axis defined the city of Beijing, with administrative buildings in the front and marketplaces at the back, the ancestral temple on the left and the altar of land and grain on the right, four temples on the four sides. In *Lüshi Chunqiu (Lü's Spring and Autumn Annals)* it is written, "The state shall be established in the middle of the world; palaces shall be built in the middle of the state; and temples shall be built in the middle of the palaces." That was the principle of the construction of Beijing. The central axis was regarded as the imperial axis, implying that one must walk up this axis before getting an audience with the emperor. According to legend, a foreign envoy refused to kneel before the Qing emperor, so officials from the Ministry of Rites led the envoy up the central axis from Zhengyang Gate through Daqing Gate, along Qianbu (Thousand-Step) Corridor and the Imperial Way. Then the diplomat was to see the golden Tian'anmen (Gate of Heavenly Peace) with its vermilion towers and white railings and the towering stone lions. Then he was ushered up through Duanmen Gate, the Wumen Gate to the Square of Taihe Palace (Palace of Supreme Harmony). The magnificent and grand imperial atmosphere awed the envoy, and he knelt in the Hall of Supreme Harmony.

Prior to the 1911 Revolution, the fortune of Beijing was closely linked to the fortune of emperors. In the Qing Dynasty, 10 emperors ruled, from Emperor Shunzhi, who began to exercise real power at the age of 14, to the last emperor Puyi, who issued the *Tuiwei Zhaoshu (Decree of Abdication)*.

Like other dynasties, there were high points during the more than 200 yearJinds of the Qing rule, such as during the reigns of emperors Kangxi and Qianlong. Like the emperors of the previous Jin and Yuan dynasties, emperors of the Qing Dynasty were great admirers of Han culture and advocated the integration of the country's different ethnic groups.

In contrast to previous dynasties, China was fairly open during the Qing Dynasty. All year round, there were European, West Asian, Indian and Arab merchants, missionaries, artists and gold diggers living in Beijing. Emperor Shunzhi, the first Qing emperor, made pioneering efforts in appointing Han officials to his government. He was also a diligent student of Han culture. In addition, he gave audience to Adam Schall, a missionary from Germany. He honoured Schall as "Grandfather" and learned astronomy and philosophy from him. Schall had high status in the court of Emperor Shunzhi, who followed his advice closely. Even his decision for choosing his heir apparent, Xuanye, was made on Schall's advice. After Emperor Shunzhi, there was a long period of peace during the reign of the Emperors Kangxi, Yongzheng and Qianlong.

The Qing Dynasty adopted the Forbidden City of Ming Dynasty and continued with the urban planning along the central axis. Creative construction took place during the reign of Emperor Qianlong. As transport was still underdeveloped at the time, the emperor had to go out of the palace to experience the everyday life of his subjects. During his lifetime, Emperor Qianlong visited the areas south of the Yangtze River six times. He would sometimes travel incognito to check the integrity of his officials. He greatly appreciated the beautiful sceneries and gardens of the south of China, which sparked his wish to bring all gardens into his capital.

During his 60-year reign, Emperor Qianlong conducted the continuous construction of Beijing. First, he expanded Yuanmingyuan (Old Summer Palace). Then he built Changchun Garden to its east and Jingyi Garden at Xiang Shan (Fragrant Hills). In 1749, he celebrated the longevity of his mother by building Qingyi Garden at Weng Shan, which are today's Wanshou Hill (Hill of Longevity) and Yiheyuan (Summer Palace). At the same time, he renovated Changchun Garden, the residence of the empress dowager. He built the West Garden for the schooling of princes. He then expanded Jingming Garden to include all Yuquan Hill. In 1760, the western-style mansion at the north of Changchun Garden was completed. In 1769, he took back the gardens for princes and princesses at the southeast of the Old Summer Palace and put them together into Yichun Garden. That marked the completion of the Beijing classic gardens. Qianlong left Beijing with dozens of architectural wonders, such as the azure glaze tiles of Qinian Palace (Palace of Prayer for Good Harvest) in the Temple of Heaven, the Summer Palace, the three gardens of the Old Summer Palace, the Fragrant Hills and Yuquan Hill. Those constructions marked the climax of imperial gardens in the Qing Dynasty. Except for the Old Summer Palace, which was burned down by the Anglo-French Allied Troops, all these constructions have become world heritage sites.

Changes came thick and fast. While flowers continued to blossom in Qianlong's gardens, the Qing Dynasty was on the brink of collapse. Finally, the last emperor Puyi abdicated at the age of six. The decree was issued by Empress Dowager Longyu who wrote, "As the people favour a republic, there were uprisings in southern and central provinces first, followed by agreement of the northern generals. A republic is the common aspiration of the country, so I will lead the emperor to give the reign of the country to the people." In his book *Twilight in the Forbidden City,* Reginald Johnston, the English teacher of Emperor Puyi, recorded the terms to which the dynasty came with the government of the Republic of China, such as the retaining of the title, the expense of 4 million silver dollars (US$1 million) for the emperor from the state budget, temporary residence in the Forbidden City followed by permanent residence in the Summer Palace as well as the retaining of servants and guards. As his ancestors, Puyi was versatile and eager to learn from both the Chinese and the West, but he was unable to bring back his empire, so the 268 years of rule of the Qing Dynasty came to an end.

As an emperor, Puyi suffered many mishaps. However, in Johnston's accounts, abdication marked the beginning of his efforts to switch from an emperor's life to that of a commoner.

Beijing, the capital of four dynasties, was the place where historic figures and heroes made their achievements and where most of them rest in peace. The legacies they left constitute the stories of the 860 years in the history of Beijing as the imperial capital. Inclusiveness was and has been the spirit of the city ever since its first day as national capital.

Rich Soil, the Land Where Dragons Hide

Gary Gygax was an insurance salesman, but his primary interest in life was gaming. In 1968, he rented a hall near his home in Lake Geneva to hold the first Lake Geneva Gaming Convention. A few years later, with partner Dave Arneson, he invented the classic role playing game, *Dungeons and Dragons*.

From the birth of *Dungeons and Dragons* in 1974 to the demise of Gygax on March 4, 2008, countless gamers and game developers became his fans. And in the East, a group of *Dungeons and Dragons* fans also believe dragons are closely related to invisible cities of another world.

After Gygax passed away, some people began to wonder if his dungeons and dragons came from western culture or a Chinese story he had read. During this discussion, a name with more than 700 years of history came up: Liu Bowen. Liu is one of the founding heroes of the Ming Dynasty (1368–1644) and deemed by some to have been one of the smartest people in the world. It is claimed he is the son of the Jade Emperor (the ruler of Heaven and all realms of existence below including the Man and Hell) and was sent to the mortal world to help Zhu Yuanzhang (reign: 1368–98), the Ming founding emperor, to unify China. It is he who tamed the evil dragons in the sea of bitterness in Youzhou and built the city of Beijing; it is also he who drove away evil dragons and selected the resting places for the 13 emperors of the Ming Dynasty. Maybe these are just stories, but what we know is that emperors of the Qing Dynasty (1644–1911) followed their Ming counterparts and built lavish tombs for themselves and their consorts around Beijing.

The imperial tombs around Beijing tell the world that Beijing is the real site of *Dungeons and Dragons*.

The Only Place for Rulers of China

In 1153, Wanyan Liang (reign: 1150–61), the emperor of the Jin Dynasty (1115–1234), moved his capital to Beijing from far away. He called Beijing "Zhongdu," the Central Capital of Jin, starting the Beijing's history as a capital.

Though Wanyan Liang was an emperor killer and a cruel warmonger, he was also devoted to Chinese culture and possessed an excellent learning ability and outstanding memory. His choice of Beijing as the capital was the result of deep research and deliberation.

Wanyan Liang consulted *fengshui* masters on the geomantic omens of Beijing as the capital. These masters usually resorted to examples in the classics of Chinese culture. For example, Yang Yiru, a geographer from the Tang Dynasty (AD 618–907), once elaborated on the geographical advantages of Beijing, and Zhu Xi from the Song Dynasty (AD 960–1279) further explained that Beijing was an auspicious location. These examples all pushed Wanyan Liang to choose Beijing as the capital.

In 2002, a mausoleum from the Jin Dynasty was unearthed in Fangshan District, Beijing. As one of the few imperial tombs of the ethnic minorities, this mausoleum is the earliest and largest of its kind in Beijing. Taking more than 60 years to finish, this tomb covers an area of 60 square kilometres. Later, the tomb of the founding emperor of the Jin Dynasty was also unearthed. Though the outer coffin was already broken, people could still find traces of the luxurious style from the precious materials used to make the coffin and other exquisite funerary objects, such as a gold phoenix coronet. To the southwest of the founding emperor's mausoleum, five more subordinate tombs were found.

The discovery of these tombs has made people aware that when Wanyan Liang was developing the economy in his new capital, he was also selecting the perfect afterlife residence for the late Jin emperors. After Wanyan Liang relocated the capital to Beijing, he decided to move the ancestral graves from Heilongjiang to Beijing. He sent the officials in charge of astronomy and the calendar to find auspicious land around Beijing and finally the location in Fangshan District was chosen. According to geomantic theories, the mountains on three sides and the ditch on one side of the location symbolised the gods of the northern sky, the eastern sky, the western sky and the southern sky, and these good omens made this place perfect for a mausoleum. He inspected the construction four times and even lived on the site for half a month to supervise the work in person. In October 1155, the mausoleum was completed. Wanyan Liang held grand rituals to relocate the graves of the late Jin emperors to this place.

The Jurchen people who founded the Jin Dynasty were brave and skilful in warfare. The dynasty is called Jin (gold) because the name of the preceding Liao Dynasty (AD 916–1125) means iron. The founding Jin emperor wanted to conquer iron with gold and bring all China under his rule; however, he did not live to see this happen. But his descendant Wanyan Liang enabled him to watch over the Jin territory in his afterlife by moving his grave to Beijing.

Chinese emperors believed they should maintain their imperial dignity in the afterlife, so the size of their tombs is symbolic of the extent of their power.

After serving as the capital for Jin, Yuan, Ming and Qing dynasties, Beijing witnessed the end of imperial rule and the birth of the republic in the Revolution of 1911. Among the four dynasties, only the Yuan Dynasty (1271–1368) does not have a record suggesting an imperial mausoleum was established in Beijing.

In fact, in selecting Beijing as the capital, Kublai Khan also undertook research and deliberation. According to the *History of the Yuan Dynasty,* a Mongolian aristocrat once told Kublai Khan one must reside in Beijing if he wanted to rule China, as Beijing had the perfect geographical condition and location. Kublai Khan took the advice and made Beijing the capital in 1264. However, with the rise of the Ming Dynasty, the Yuan capital vanished along with the dynasty it served. The real dragon, or the true son of heaven from the Jin Dynasty was buried underground in Beijing, but its Yuan counterparts must be wandering in some alien land.

Origin of the Imperial House and Capital of Emperors

During the Jin and Yuan dynasties, Beijing was a promising land, as it was a place where emperors could establish their empires not only for themselves but also for their successors. After the Ming Dynasty established its rule with Nanjing as the capital, Emperor Yongle (reign: 1402–24) fought his way to the throne. He was not interested in Nanjing as the capital, so his ministers began to plan for a new capital.

There are two legends, both involving an arrow. For the people of Nanjing, the favourite legend is the "selection of Beijing by Xu Da's arrow." When the emperor asked his ministers about the site of the new capital, Xu Da, at the recommendation of ministers, shot an arrow to the north and it landed at the site of the new capital. Xu Da's arrow is said to have landed in the very centre of Beijing, so the legend is also popular among Beijingers. It is said that when he was pacifying the north of China, Zhu Di, as the ambitious King of Yan, began to look for the site of his future capital. Regardless of who shot the arrow, the place where it actually fell is still in dispute. People in Zhao County and Anguo County of Hebei Province believed that it landed there, rather than Beijing.

There is a passage in the *Historical Records of the Ming Dynasty—the Records of Emperor Taizong:* "Beijing, as the origin of your majesty, is encircled by Juyong Pass to the north, Taihang Mountain to the west, Shanhai Pass to the east and the Central Plains to the south. It is in a position to control the whole empire, so it is an excellent choice for a capital." That is a reasonable opinion, supported by the analyses of the Jin and Yuan dynasties as well as previous dynasties. Throughout history, scholars studied the geography, environment and customs of Beijing and reached the view that Beijing is very suitable for human residence, since it was well-positioned, rich in natural resources and was a biological balance.

Like Wanyan Liang of the Jin Dynasty, Emperor Chengzu of the Ming Dynasty began to look for a site for his tomb immediately after entering Beijing. That thought may seem unreasonable today. When unsure of where their souls might go after death, people have different attitudes towards their afterlife. Some hope to enjoy peace and happiness in the afterlife while others concentrate solely on this life. Emperors and their families, who believed that they enjoyed divine rights, hoped to enjoy the same life and luxury in the afterlife. That is the reason for the lavish and magnificent tombs, and the Ming Tombs are no exception.

In a 40-square-kilometre basin at the southern foot of the Tianshou Mountain in Changping District, are the 13 Ming Tombs; namely Changling, Xianling, Jingling, Yuling, Maoling, Tailing, Kangling, Yongling, Zhaoling, Dingling, Qingling, Deling and Siling tombs. Emperor Zhengtong (reign: 1436–49; 1457–64), who is the sixth emperor in Ming Dynasty and became emperor by way of a coup, was not buried beside his ancestors, but at the foot of the Yuquan Mountain in the west of Beijing. His mausoleum was named Jingtai Tomb. The Ming Tombs at the foot of the Tianshou Mountain and the Jingtai Tomb are the best-preserved imperial tombs in China.

In 1368, Zhu Yuanzhang overthrew the Yuan Dynasty and established the Ming Dynasty. After becoming emperor, he followed traditions by upholding Confucianism and righteousness in politics. In the Ming Dynasty, there were stringent rules on tombs for officials. Zhu Yuanzhang's tomb is in Nanjing. It is guarded by stone sculptures of human and animal figures at the front. Behind the Ling'en Palace, the commemoration place, lies a huge raised area above the tomb. In the shape of a round castle, it is called "pearl fortress." In front of the pearl fortress is a huge platform on which stands a square castle. This arrangement became the standard for tombs of the Ming rulers. In 1409, Emperor Yongle, moved the capital to Beijing and began building his palace and searching for a site for his tomb. He selected the location in Changping District, which he named the Underground Palace of the Dingling Tomb. The main structure was finished in 1413 and Empress Xu was buried there. In 1424, the emperor himself died during an expedition to the north and was buried together with his wife in this tomb.

As a historical world heritage site, the Ming Tombs have been preserved and studied in detail. In 1950, the newly founded PRC conducted preservation work on the tombs. In 1955, the Ming Tombs were put under the administration of the Beijing Municipal Government, which sent a construction team to renovate the Changling, Jingling and Yongling tombs. In 1957, the Ming Tombs were included in the first group of key cultural relic sites under protection in Beijing. In 1961, they were included in the list of the key national cultural relic sites under protection. In June 1981, the Office of the Ming Tombs was set up and it invested the tourism revenues into the renovation of the Deling, Kangling, Qingling and Tailing tombs. In 1982, the Badaling and the Ming Tombs Area was included in the list of 44 key national scenic areas by the State Council. In 1991, the Ming Tombs were designated as one of the "40 Excellent Tourist Attractions in China." In 1992, the Ming Tombs were honoured as the best preserved mausoleum cluster with the most emperors buried in the world, by the Selection Committee of the Best Tourist Attractions in Beijing. In 2003, the Ming Tombs were recognised by UNESCO as a world heritage site. Renovation plans for the Yuling and Maoling tombs, which have not been renovated since the reign of Emperor Qianlong of the Qing Dynasty, were written in the *Medium to Long-Term Renovation and Preservation Plan (2008–2015)*, which was submitted in June 2010.

Until now, the Dingling Tomb is the only one excavated. From 1956 to 1958, archaeologists explored the underground palace and many cultural relics were excavated. Since then, the other tombs have been kept intact, since both Xia Nai, the leading archaeologist in China, and Zheng Zhenduo, a writer and historian, advocated the deferment of excavation because of insufficient technology in preservation after excavation. As a result, there have been many legends about the secrets buried in those tombs. According to Luo Zhewen, an expert of ancient architecture, "The Ming Tombs have high architectural value. The *nanmu* building of the Changling Tomb is the largest in China. The stone sculpture is delicate. The tombs serve as a showcase of architectural achievement in the Ming Dynasty."

Beautiful scenery at the Ming Tombs still attracted tourists. It is said that the Tianshou Mountain is the dragon vein of Beijing, meaning the emperors who rest there have remained with their treasured capital.

Auspicious Sites for Imperial Tombs

The power of the Han culture can be best seen in the politics, economy and culture of the Yuan and Qing dynasties. Numerous historical records show that the Qing emperors had been influenced by the Ming Tombs when they built their own tombs.

During the reign of the first two emperors of the Qing Dynasty, China was not unified. Both emperors understood that Manchurians should assimilate the advanced Han culture if they wanted to rule the whole country. They appointed former Ming ministers as high officials and learned the laws and regulations of the Ming Dynasty. In 1644, Emperor Shunzhi (reign: 1643–61) stormed through the Shanhai Pass and occupied the whole country. He inherited the Ming Dynasty system and palace. He was also inspired by the Ming Tombs. It is said that he chose the Yan Mountain in the eastern suburbs of Beijing as the site of his mausoleum during a hunting tour. Later, the tombs for his empress and for Emperor Kangxi were built in the same area. These are the Eastern Qingling Tombs in today's Zunhua County of Hebei Province. These tombs were built in the same form as the Ming Tombs, with independent tombs forming a unified cluster. The current eastern Qing Tombs include the Xiaoling Tomb of Emperor Shunzhi, the Jingling Tomb of Emperor Kangxi (reign: 1662–1722), the Yuling Tomb of Emperor Qianlong, the Dingling Tomb of Emperor Xianfeng, the Huiling Maosoleum of Emperor Tongzhi, four tombs for empresses, including Ci'an and Cixi, five tombs for concubines and one tomb for a princess. In total, 14 empresses and 136 concubines were buried there.

In Chinese history, stories about coups within the imperial family are numerous. There is one about Emperor Yongzheng (reign: 1722–35) of the Qing Dynasty. Legend has it that he seized the throne by tampering with his father's edict. People use the story to explain the fact that Emperor Yongzheng built his tomb in Yixian County, Hebei Province, rather than with the others. He did not want to be reprimanded by his father in the afterlife. The site of the western Qing Tombs is excellent. According to the *Travelogue of the Yongning Mountain* by Sun Dinglie of the Qing Dynasty, "The site is enclosed by the Taihang Mountains." The place boasts the largest pine forest in North China, with more than 20,000 pine trees over an area of 8,000 hectares. The Emperors' Valley built here was probably the idea of Emperor Yongzheng at the advice of his courtiers and ministers. The western Qing Tombs include four emperor's tombs; the Tailing Tomb of Emperor Yongzheng, the Changling Tomb of Emperor Jiaqing, the Muling Tomb of Emperor Daoguang and the Chongling Tomb of Emperor Guangxu. There are three tombs for empresses; the Taidong, Changxi and Mudong tombs, as well as three tombs for concubines; the Taifei, Changfei and Chongfei tombs. In addition, there are 14 tombs for princes and princesses. In 1995, the ashes of the last emperor, Puyi (1906–1967), were buried here.

In both the Ming Tombs and the eastern and western Qing Tombs, imperial palaces were replicated so that emperors may continue their reign in the afterlife.

Among the emperors, empresses and concubines, Empress Dowager Cixi is the most significant, as she was the de facto ruler during the reign of two emperors. According to the laws of the Qing Dynasty, the tomb of an empress who died after her husband should be smaller than that of her husband. However, Empress Dowager Cixi ignored this requirement. Her tomb ranks first among the Qing Tombs in terms of size, cost and luxury.

The luxury of Cixi's tomb exceeds that of the Forbidden City, with priceless mortuary

objects. According to Li Lianying, the chief eunuch at her death, "Three layers of gold filaments and one layer of pearls were laid in the coffin before the body was placed in it. Jade lotus leaves were laid at her head and jasper lotus flowers were laid at her feet. An egg-sized pearl costing 500,000 kilograms of silver decorated her crown and 27 Buddhist figures made of gold, jewels and jade were set beside her body. Beside her feet were jadeite watermelon, muskmelon, cabbage and over 200 gemstone peaches, plums, apricots and dates. On her left was a jade lotus flower and on her right was a jade coral. In addition, there were eight jade horses and 18 jade arhats. Altogether there were more than 700 objects. After the funeral, four litres of pearls and 2,200 gemstones were poured into the coffin." In 1928, those treasures were looted by the warlord Sun Dianying. Most have never been recovered.

From today's perspective, Empress Dowager Cixi had a unique personality. The plan of her tomb was changed three times. As a result of her desire for luxury, her tomb became a cultural heritage for posterity. In this tomb, the columns, doors and windows of the Ling'en Palace were all made of rose wood and *nanmu*. Pictures of dragons, phoenixes, clouds and longevity symbols were painted on the beams. The 2,400 golden dragons painted on the murals are still glittering today. Thirty stone panels with carvings symbolising happiness and longevity decorate the walls of the three rooms inside the building. The railings on the base of the Ling'en Palace are carved with dragons and phoenixes. A total of 138 images of phoenixes and dragons are carved on both sides of the 69 panels. On the 74 column caps, there are sculptures of phoenixes flying through the clouds. On the column are carvings of dragons emerging from the water. As recorded in the film *Administering from Behind a Curtain,* the young Cixi was very ambitious, as she wanted the phoenix to be above the dragon. The sculptures and carvings in her mausoleum show that she was the only one in the 276 years of the Qing Dynasty who could achieve her desire. The final phase of the Qing Dynasty was marked by female supremacy.

Finding Life in Opera

The scene was a prison. A man called Andy tied up the prison guards and occupied the room where prisoners were given orders. He put on a record and *The Marriage of Figaro* echoed through the sky above the prison. Anyone who has seen *The Shawshank Redemption* will not forget this scene. "That's a moment of freedom. After so many years, I still have fresh memories about this moment," Tim Robbins, who played Andy Dufresne, said in an interview in 2005, 10 years after the movie was first shown.

In 1815, Napoleon lost power after the Battle of Waterloo and was imprisoned on the island of Saint Helena. He had six years there to recall his experiences and struggles from his life. It is said that Napoleon deeply missed the days when he enjoyed going to the opera in Paris. That was the sound he loved and remembered, and which always remained with him.

Sometimes, history is a cage. Many bewildering changes and great events are preserved in historical materials and relics that people now can see and touch despite so many years having passed. Over solid and substantial historical facts floats a kind of music that persists long after the events have passed. People in later generations compare opera to a melody of the reed pipe. You can feel the tender and gentle veins of the music that lingers in your memory like silk fibres. You can explore the vicissitudes of life that actors and actresses perform on the stage. All these can be traced back to the truth in the ancient and modern histories of a city. You might vaguely see that, no matter what fortunes or hardships cities and people experienced through different dynasties, they would often find life in opera.

Beijing, a city with 860 years of history as a capital, is also a capital of opera.

Weapons Laid Down, Armour Discarded

Beijing first became China's capital 860 years ago during the Jin Dynasty (1115–1234). But it was a short tenure compared with the later Yuan (1271–1368), Ming (1368–1644) and Qing (1644–1911) dynasties. It was Wanyan Liang, also known as the King Hailing and the deposed emperor of the Jin Dynasty, who coveted the capital of the former Yan Kingdom. He marched his troops into Beijing and built Zhongdu (Central Capital), capital of the Jin Dynasty. He started many construction projects and built the city in a style befitting a state capital in a prosperous age. At the same time, he and his subjects, members of the Nüzhen ethnic minority, had a thirst for the culture of the Han people. In fact, later generations of the Jin Dynasty all studied Han culture.

They learnt the written language of the Han people, read their books and dressed in the Han style. They also promoted and used the Han methods of social management and education.

In the film *Farewell My Concubine*, the manager of the Xiliancheng Training Troupe spanks a little apprentice with a feather duster and tells him to learn opera earnestly. He says, "A person will listen to opera as long as he is human." It is no exaggeration if we apply this sentence to the period of the Jin Dynasty when Emperor Zhangzong held the throne. At the time, the *yuanben* opera of the Jin Dynasty was developing toward *zaju* opera. Then there appeared a dramatist named Dong Xieyuan, who had an indelibly profound influence on the development of opera in later generations. His masterpiece was *Xixiangji (Romance of the West Chamber).*

From its birth until now, many genres of drama have adapted *Romance of the West Chamber*, the opera was changed and added to, it has reached many people, and many artists have performed it… In 2012, the North Kunqu Opera Theatre, which represented the highest standard of Kunqu opera in Beijing, performed *Romance of the West Chamber* at the John F. Kennedy Centre for the Performing Arts in Washington D.C. By the end of the same year, composer Bai Xianyong staged a hall version of the opera that was noted for its fashionable presentation. News appeared constantly about the *Romance of the West Chamber* and the opera was shown on the stage. However, these were all latecomers. The *Romance of the West Chamber* that modern people are the most familiar with is actually "Wang's *Romance of the West Chamber*," the version by Wang Shifu, a dramatist of the Yuan Dynasty. However, a version pre-dating Wang's that possesses more epochal spiritual meaning because it describes love and criticises feudal male power, and which has a complete structure of drama and is the closest to modern drama, is "Dong's *Romance of the West Chamber*," from the Jin Dynasty.

Very little is known about Dong Xieyuan's life. Some say the two characters, Xieyuan, are honorific for intellectuals, and not his actual name. Most historical materials seem to agree that he was liberal, talented and had an exceptional ability to control language and story structure. The full name for "Dong's *Romance of the West Chamber*" is *Xixiangji Zhugong Ci (Various Gong Tones for the Romance of the West Chamber)*.

The time when Dong Xieyuan lived was an age of peace and prosperity. There were many entertainment facilities where performers gathered. These places were similar in many ways to today's. The performers would tell stories or put on variety shows. At the time, *yuanben* opera was very popular. Humorous plays, which combined storytelling with vaudeville and variety acts, evolved from more formal opera works that combined singing and spoken words. The performance of *yuanben* opera developed not only the performance structure of having the first and second consecutive scenes arranged according to plot, but also relatively complete roles and role types. The popular *yuanben* opera pieces were mostly about historical and romantic themes, particularly the difficulties and hardships of common people, and mocked those who held power and criticised current political affairs. It was recorded in *Chuo Geng Lu (Records of Tillage Leisure)*, by Tao Zongyi in the Ming Dynasty, that there were some 700 *yuanben* operas, but most of these works have been lost.

Zhang Dai's words, in fact, only apply to Dong Xieyuan's *Romance of the West Chamber*. When examined today, "Dong's *Romance of the West Chamber*" still shows magnificent structure. The development in the drama shows great originality and the plots feature flowing and striking climaxes. Of particular value in "Dong's *Romance of the West Chamber*" are its combination of speaking and singing, more melodies and less talk, and beautiful language. Its creation is rooted in folk literature and art. It put together the vocabulary with rich expressive force in poetry and folk colloquial language to form a simple and solid style. There are still many strains in "Dong's *Romance of the West Chamber*" that are sung today.

The drama of the Jin Dynasty, represented by "Dong's *Romance of the West Chamber*" directly led to the rise to prominence of *zaju* opera in the Yuan Dynasty. It also helped Wang Shifu, a dramatist who was the next to "stand on the shoulders of giants" to write the love story of Zhang Sheng and Cui Yingying in his great masterpiece, *Romance of the West Chamber*.

Ancient Buildings Recorded Ups and Downs

The major contribution of the Yuan Dynasty is its golden capital, from which Beijing was developed. Regrettably, there are almost no traces left of the Yuan Dynasty in Beijing, except Yuan Dadu City Wall Relic Park in Chaoyang District. The disappearance of the original buildings was probably inevitable, and people now can only imagine the grandeur of the capital through historical records and the accounts of foreign travellers, such as *The Travels of Marco Polo*. Ironically, it is still disputed whether Marco Polo actually saw the scenes recorded in his book, or whether he heard about them from other travellers.

Yuanqu opera was popular in the Yuan Dynasty. It originated from folkloric lyrics and was called a "neighbourhood tune" or "village tune." Yuanqu opera combined drama and poetry, which were both popular among the people. Some scholars regard Yuanqu Opera as the drama of Yuan. Despite academic disagreements on this point, one thing everyone agrees on is the art of plays reached a peak in the capital of Yuan.

The heyday of *zaju* opera came on the heels of *jinyuanben* (Jin verse) and *Zhugong Diao* (*zhugong* tune). By incorporating various forms of performance art, including verse, drama and storytelling from the Tang and Song dynasties, *zaju* opera became a mature art form. Those dramatic verses, written by both famous writers and unknown artists, reflected the everyday life of the time, in the same way modern literary works served the purpose of preaching socialism and serving the people.

There is uncertainty about how many works of *zaju* opera still exist today. According to the most popular source, there are 500 works by Yuan writers, 50 works by anonymous writers from the period and 187 works written by anonymous writers during the transition from the Yuan to Ming dynasties: altogether, 737 works. The most prominent writers were the "Big Four": Ma Zhiyuan, Guan Hanqing, Zheng Guangzu and Bai Pu.

In a small hamlet in today's Jiuyuan Village, Wangping Town, Mentougou District, there stands a house originating from Yuan Dynasty. It is said this used to be the residence of Ma Zhiyuan. Jiuyuan Village is located on Wangping Gudao (Wangping Ancient Path), a branch of Jingxi Gudao (Jingxi Ancient Path), which is now a sightseeing attraction. The residence of Ma Zhiyuan is a large quadruple courtyard. The scene was vividly described in his work, *Tianjingsha–Qiu Si (Tianjingsha, Sentiments in Autumn)*: "Crows perching on dying branches in an old tree; stream flowing under a bridge that leads to a house; a lean horse standing in the west wind on a path; a homesick man travelling in a remote village sees the setting sun."

Though it is unclear where Ma Zhiyuan came from, people in Beijing regard him as a man from the Yuan capital. He wrote 15 dramas, of which *Hangong Qiu (Autumn in a Han Palace)* is the most representative. He also composed 120 verses, which were collected in *Dong Li Yue Fu (Anthology of the East Fence)*. Typically for a learned man at the time, he aspired to make a contribution to the country. After ups and downs in his youth, he passed the state examination in his middle age and worked his way up to be the minister of construction. In his late years, he was unhappy with the current political environment, so he retired to the countryside to enjoy drama. He was described as "the champion of drama" in poems written by the critic Jia Zhongming during the transition from the Yuan to Ming eras.

Another major dramatist closely linked to Beijing is regarded as China's top playwright and has had profound influence in the world. He is Guan Hanqing. According to historical records, he wrote 67 plays, 18 of which still exist. There are still disagreements over the authorship of some of the plays. His main works are *Dou E Yuan (The Grievance of Dou E)*, *Jiu Feng Chen (The Salvage in Hard Times)*, *Wang Jiang Ting (The Pavilion with a River View)*, *Bai Yue Ting (The Pavilion of the Moon)*, *Lu Zhailang*, *Dan Dao Hui (The Solitary Visit)* and *Tiao Feng Yue (Flirtations)*, which are still performed today. In 1958, he was honoured as a famous literary figure by the World Peace Council and activities commemorating his 700th anniversary were held all over the world. On the evening of June 28 that year, his plays were performed in 100 theatrical forms by 1,500 troupes across China. His works have been translated into English, French, German and Japanese, and he has been dubbed the "Shakespeare of the East."

Hamlet is arguably Shakespeare's best-known play, while for Guan Hanqing, that honour would go to *The Grievances of Dou E*. Dou E comes from a poor family and is sold several times before she is executed unjustly, which causes snow to fall in June. Guan Hanqing wrote the play in a sentimental yet profound manner. The desperate cry of the disillusioned Dou E has become a classic in theatrical history, "Virtuous people are poor and die young, while villains enjoy wealth and longevity. You, unjust heaven, do not stand for justice!" The grievances of Dou E symbolise the perseverance of the people in real life in the face of hardships. Most *zaju* opera express unhappiness and anger, which is the natural consequence of living under the rule of outside conquerors. The theme of *The Grievances of Dou E* is the questioning of society as a whole.

Thanks to those great playwrights, *zaju* opera brought the theatre as an art form in China to maturity. It established the standard form of four parts led by an introduction that was followed for over a century. The style of "solo followed by monologues and dialogues at intervals" set a model for later theatrical forms. The focus on stage performance, characterisation and the interaction of theme and reality had profound influence on later playwrights.

Folkloric Legends Featuring Nature and Love

After the rule of Emperor Yuanhui fled to the Mongolian grasslands, Beijing was once again under the rule of an empire established by Han people. Verses and dramas which had been highly acclaimed in the Yuan Dynasty, especially those by the Big Four, were still performed on stages in Beijing. Despite hardships and uncertainties, people still enjoyed drama, either as a celebration of peace and prosperity or entertainment in the midst of sorrow and adversity.

The history of Ming drama can be divided into two periods: from the establishment of the empire to the reign of Emperors Zhengde (1505–21) and Jiajing (1521–67), which saw the decline of *zaju* opera; and after the reign of Emperor Jiajing, which witnessed the growth of *chuanqi* opera.

Zaju opera in the early Ming Dynasty repeated its development from the Yuan Dynasty, gradually becoming the major form of entertainment on the basis of economic recovery and development. However, during the reign of Emperor Yongle, performances of *zaju* opera drew the attention of the authorities. In 1411, regulations were issued by the central government that placed strict limits on what could be performed. Actors could not perform roles of emperors, empresses, concubines, ministers, martyrs, nobles, sages or deities. Violators were subject to a punishment of 100 lashes. As a result, dramas in the early Ming Dynasty were merely pedagogical plays preaching virtue, historical plays and hollow fantasy plays, a far cry from the *zaju* opera of the Jin Dynasty, which expressed the wishes of the people and exposed the dark side of society. Drama ceased to be the carrier of popular emotions, wishes and grievances, and went into decline.

However, as one form of drama was banned, another form emerged. As drama became the pedagogical tool of governors, playwrights found a new outlet for their emotions in *chuanqi* opera. After the reign of Emperor Jiajing, Beijing became the centre of *chuanqi* opera, which attracted many excellent plays from the south of China.

In form, *chuanqi* opera in the Ming Dynasty was more complete than *zaju* opera. A play usually consisted of about 30 scenes, in two acts. Thus the structure was more compact and neat. Various tones of music were arranged in accordance with the plot. All performers could sing on the stage. Many local styles were used in the plays, in particular, *kunshan* style and *yiyang* style. After reforms by Wei Liangfu during the reign of Emperor Jiajing, *kunshan* style became the delicate and fluent *Jie* (*shuimo* tune), characterised by a complete orchestra of string, wind and percussion instruments. The staging of *Huansha Ji (The Story of Washing Silk)* spread *kunshan* style across the country and was the basis for what became Kunqu opera, which is now a world intangible cultural heritage.

After the reign of Emperor Jiajing, *chuanqi* opera became dominant in China. It reached a climax during the reign of Emperor Wanli (reign: 1600–1620), with various forms emerging. Tang Xianzu was the most prominent playwright at the time. His four masterpieces, *Zichai Ji (Story of Purple Ribbon)*, *Mudan Ting (Peony Pavilion)*, *Handan Ji (Story of Handan)* and *Nanke Ji (Story of Nanke)*, were known as "the Four Dreams of Yuming Hall." Of the four, *Peony Pavilion* is the best known. It is not a tragedy, but a story full of the joy of love and enjoyment of youthful life. It is about a girl named Du Liniang, who dies for love but is later resurrected. *Peony Pavilion* replaced the *Romance of the West Chamber* as the most popular and influential love story on stage in China, according to *Guqu Zayan (Critics on Dramas)*.

"Love flowers and grasses, and you can persevere through the vicissitudes of life." Those lines of Du Liniang in *Peony Pavilion* are still popular today. In 1986, *Peony Pavilion* was adapted as a film by Nanjing Film Studio, followed by later adaptations into *Shaoxing* opera, television series, ballet, a Kunqu opera performed internationally by the North Kunqu Opera Troupe and film by Chinese Mainland and Hong Kong companies. Over the centuries, the story of *Peony Pavilion* has been the favourite theme of performances from imperial theatres to village stages.

The prosperity of *chuanqi* opera lingered on into the Qing Dynasty, and its popularity among different classes of society paved the way for the emergence and growth of Beijing opera.

Huidiao and Handiao Combined to Create Beijing Opera

Each dynasty in history has left its distinctive drama. Theatrical masters and playwrights left their marks by probing into the interaction between drama, history and life.

Chuanqi opera retained its dominance at the transition from the Ming to Qing dynasties. Kunqu was popular, but its southern style restricted its development in Beijing, which was awaiting a truly national drama.

Fast forward to 1790 and entertainers in Beijing were preparing for the 80th birthday celebration for Emperor Qianlong. Along a five-kilometre parade route from Xihuamen Gate to Gaoliang Bridge outside Xizhimen Gate, there was a stage every 20 metres. There were performances by theatre troupes from all over the country. One of these was Sanqing Huiban Troupe, led by Gao Langting, a performer from Anqing, and it led to the creation of what is today one of the world's best known forms of opera. Huiban troupes sang *huidiao*, which was a combination of *xipi* and *erhuang*. This later became the main tune of Beijing opera. Combining *huidiao* with *handiao* and local Beijing tunes to create a new form of opera was the Anhui and Hubei troupes' greatest contribution to opera's development. The new opera immediately attracted audiences in Beijing and that year is regarded as the beginning of Beijing opera.

Like all dramas in history,

Beijing opera originated from the grass roots of society. However, its development was different. Unlike other dramas that matured in public theatres, the growth of Beijing opera was driven by the imperial family.

Most members of the imperial family in the Qing Dynasty were opera fans and many of them were also good at creating operas. According to records of the Qing Dynasty, Nanfu and Jingshan, offices in charge of performances at court, were established no later than the reign of Emperor Kangxi (1661–1722). Actors performing at court were sponsored by the government and they were mostly outstanding artists, such as master Beijing opera performers Tan Xinpei, Wang Yaoqing and Yang Xiaolou.

Emperor Xianfeng (reign: 1850–61) was the first to admit Beijing opera into the palace. He often ordered performances and sometimes directed performances by eunuchs. Empress Dowager Cixi was also a great fan and she watched performances every day. On April 25, 2013, the Garden of Virtuous Harmony (Deheyuan) in the Summer Palace (Yiheyuan) was reopened after 18 months of renovation. This imperial opera theatre was built in the late Qing period and was originally for Cixi's exclusive use. The three-storey opera building alone cost 710,000 silver pieces. The garden symbolised that Beijing opera had been fully embraced by the palace. It also served as the link between the palace and the people, with folk artists improving their performances outside the palace after being honoured inside it.

Cixi was a significant figure in the development of Beijing opera. According to historical records, she held scripts while watching opera so she could check the actors' performances. Her comments and criticisms were always accurate. She also directed the adaptation of plays. After returning the administration of the empire to Emperor Guangxu, she moved to the Summer Palace and ordered the adaptation of *Zhao Dai Xiao Shao* into Beijing opera. According to the memoirs of Wang Yaoqing, the "godfather" of Beijing opera, he developed his ability to create new tunes for lyrics under the pressure from Cixi. From May 7-16, 2013, *Zhao Dai Xiao Shao*, the opera created by Cixi, was performed for 10 days at Chang'an Grand Theatre in Beijing. This was the first authentic imperial Beijing opera adapted from a Qing palace opera.

The ban issued by Ming palace led to the decline of drama, while the support by the Qing palace caused the maturing and development of Beijing opera. Various troupes emerged in Beijing, with professional academies led by masters. Thanks to the continuous efforts by generations of opera masters, on November 16, 2010, Beijing opera was finally included in the Representative List of Human Intangible Cultural Heritages after a unanimous vote by the 24 member states of the Intergovernmental Committee for UNESCO's Protection of Intangible Cultural Heritages. Beijing opera is thus a cultural symbol of Beijing as well as China.

Over the 860 years since it became the capital of the Jin Dynasty, Beijing has played a significant role in the development of drama and opera in China. A millennium of theatrical performances has shaped the cultural identity of Beijing. All forms of drama, from *jinyuanben* and *zaju* opera to *chuanqi*, Kunqu and Beijing opera, originated from Beijing and attained national dominance. Literati and intellectuals in Beijing helped to upgrade and refine various forms of drama and opera, making them grand in style, profound in theme and delicate in expression. Beijing is truly the capital of drama and opera.

Painting, Dance of Colours

His name is always among the first mentioned when the subject of modern European art is raised. His painting "Woman Reading" was bought by a Chinese collector for US$21.3 million at Sotheby's 2012 spring auction. He became a member of the French Communist Party in 1944 and then, in 1945, he was featured in the *Jiefang Daily*, published in Yan'an, China. He is the artist Pablo Picasso. And it was Picasso who opened the door of his villa to the Chinese painter Chang Dai-chien on July 29, 1956. That day, Chang saw Picasso studying Chinese painting and was surprised by the long-lasting and profound influence of Chinese art when Picasso said, "When it comes to art in the world, it's the Chinese people who have art in the first place. Why do so many Chinese people come to Paris to study art?" A later biography of Chang Dai-chien documented his thoughts on this. He originally believed Picasso was simply being modest and polite towards his Chinese guest but, on examining the Chinese-style exercises his host had done, he began to realise Picasso was truly fascinated by Chinese painting.

Throughout history, we find support for Picasso's compliment. When young Italian explorer Marco Polo came to the Chinese capital in the 13th century, he commented that paintings on silk by Chinese artists looked like a "dance of colours." In 2012, Li Keran's "Wanshanhongbian" ("Thousands of Hills in a Crimsoned View") was sold for 293.25 million yuan (US$47.3 million), a record high for a Chinese work at auction. However, when following the path covered by Chinese painters of all generations, we can trace the origin of their painting skills back to the local painting skills of China. Beijing is home to many painting masters, who have written an exceptional history of China and its brilliant capital city.

Wild Scenes from Home are Nothing More Than Worship of Han Chinese Culture

There are six horse sculptures standing before the mausoleum of Tang Dynasty Emperor Taizong Li Shimin (AD 599–649): "Sa Lu Zi," "Quan Mao Ju," "Bai Ti Wu," "Te Le Biao," "Qing Zhui" and "Shi Fa Chi." The six horses were Li Shimin's favourite battle steeds, astride which he recorded many victories. Today, if you visit the Palace Museum (Forbidden City), you can see Zhao Lin's Jin Dynasty (1115–1234) masterpiece: "The Six Steeds of Zhao Mausoleum." The original six stone sculptures were done using the technique and Zhao Lin has used this as his main source in generating style and movement in his painting. This is a rarely seen masterpiece of horse painting from the Jin Dynasty (1115–1234). In 1959, China's State Administration of Cultural Heritage of the Ministry of Culture allocated the painting to the Palace Museum for collection. As things stand, no specific historical data remains about the painter's life. The only hint comes from the preface and postscript at the bottom of the work, written by Zhao Bingwen from the Jin Dynasty. It indicates Zhao Lin might have been a native of Luoyang who was recruited to the imperial palace because of his excellence in painting during the reign of Emperor Shizong (1123–1189) of the Jin Dynasty. "The Six Steeds of Zhao Mausoleum" is his only known extant work.

Jin Dynasty paintings reflect the integration of the art of minorities and the Han Chinese culture. The ruggedness rooted in a dynasty formed by an ethnic minority coming to power in Beijing became refined as the dynasty gradually stabilised and entered a short-term period of peace. The Jin Dynasty valued painting and a painting bureau was established under the curator of the imperial library. All paintings plundered from the imperial storehouse of the Song Dynasty (AD 960–1279) were stored in the painting bureau so they could be studied by the nobility and court painters. As a result, the painting of the Jin Dynasty was greatly influenced by that of the Song Dynasty. That being said, the spiritual "home" of the minority, that of valuing horses, determined that its paintings inevitably featured themes showing national character, whether fine horses running like the wind, the bitter cold beyond the Great Wall, or turbulent rivers and precipitous cliffs. The painting style is that of the Han people, yet it also invokes a feeling nourished by white mountains and black water.

"Wenjiguihan Tujuan," a painting by an artist known only by his family name, Zhang, collected in the Jilin Provincial Museum, is representative of Jin painting art. It is the artist's only known work, and it is assumed that he lived in the period of Emperor Zhangzong (1168–1208) of the Jin Dynasty. It describes the scene where Cai Wenji, a woman of the late Han Dynasty, and her entourage move forward amid harsh conditions and a gale from the northern desert. There are numerous figures in the picture with a clear-cut distinction between the important and the lesser ones. The description of their expressions is vivid and precise. Although the environment isn't touched upon, the portrayal of the figures highlights the long journey and bitter cold and wind.

"Chibi Tu" the ink-on-paper wash painting of Wu Yuanzhi, also of the Jin Dynasty, is enshrined in Taipei's National Palace Museum. Once, there was considerable dispute over whether it was produced during the Jin Dynasty, as it showed the romantic charm of paintings of the Song Dynasty. So, with Jin painting, even the torrential momentum of a great wave crashing had reached the point where it reflected the scholarly elegance and spirit of the Han people.

Few paintings of the Jin Dynasty are preserved today. In 1214, the Jin Dynasty moved its capital to Kaifeng, Henan Province and named it Nanjing (southern capital). Later, the Mongol cavalry burned the former capital to the ground, totally destroying the city. Nobody knows how many priceless treasures and works of art were destroyed, which makes the fewer than ten surviving paintings of the Jin Dynasty all the more valuable.

Masterful Depiction of Rain and Clouds over Mountains

When the Mongols wiped out the Jin Dynasty, they brought a golden era to Beijing. Although historical records are generally sober and dry, they are unanimous in using poetic words to praise the grandeur of Dadu (where Beijing now stands) of the Yuan Dynasty (1271–1368), the capital city that attracted the attention of the world. It is probably because of its beauty and charm that Dadu had to be destroyed later and therefore give wings to people's imagination with respect to its past glory.

Times of prosperity and peace give rise to official-scholars, artists and men of letters. Dadu, the capital city of the Yuan Dynasty, was a particularly wonderful place for artists. At the beginning of the Yuan Dynasty, artists, especially

Chinese artists, enjoyed great freedom in their life and work. The Mongol rulers, who were erstwhile nomadic and not sophisticated in education and culture, wanted to learn Chinese culture, in particular, the Confucian classics, to consolidate their rule over the new empire. Kublai Khan (1215–94), or Yuan Emperor Shizu, recruited many Chinese intellectuals to his government. Emperor Renzong (1285–1320) and Emperor Wenzong (1304–32) were great patrons of literature and art. Emperor Wenzong even appointed painters and calligraphers to appraise works of painting and calligraphy in his newly-established Kuizhangge.

The openness of the society brings the opportunity for artists to develop their own styles and display their personalities through their works. Literati painting became the mainstream of this period. Except for a few professional painters who served in the palace, most Yuan Dynasty painters were officials or literati, who enjoyed depicting their own living environment, interests and ambitions, and subject matters such as mountains, rivers, trees, bamboos, rocks, orchids and plums were found in many of their paintings. Compared with the Jin Dynasty, there were fewer paintings depicting social life. Instead, more emphasis was put on the literary taste, the skilful use of brushes and ink, and the combination of calligraphy, poetry and painting. In the history of Chinese painting, the Yuan Dynasty is regarded as a period when the ancient traditions were revived but new styles were created. It had significant influence on the artistic creations of the Ming and Qing dynasties.

Dadu remained as the centre of painting in China until the end of the Yuan Dynasty. As it fell into decline, the centre of painting shifted to the Yangtze River Delta. During the early Yuan Dynasty, painting arts flourished in Dadu. There emerged a number of renowned imperial painters such as He Cheng, Liu Guandao, Li Xiaoyan and Liu Yuan. They carried forward the traditions of the Song (AD 960–1279) and Jin dynasties in portrait and religious painting. The one painter who initiated the new style for Yuan Dynasty was Zhao Mengfu, a descendant of the imperial house of the Song Dynasty.

Zhao Mengfu, who called himself Zi'ang or Songxue, was a direct descendant of Zhao Kuangyin, Emperor Taizu (AD 927–976) of the Song Dynasty. Zhao Mengfu's father worked as the Vice-Minister of Revenue and the Governor of Zhexi, Lin'an in the Song Dynasty.

After the fall of the Song, he retired to the countryside. However, as the saying goes, gold glitters wherever it is. When Yuan Emperor Chengzong (1265–1307) wanted to compile *The Records of Emperor Shizu*, Zhao Mengfu was summoned to the court, because he was famous for his achievements in poetry, calligraphy, painting, music, sculpture and administration. The emperor insisted that he stay even after he requested for retirement on the pretext of illness. In 1316, he was promoted to be a highest-ranking official, however, he remains a controversial figure because of his defection to the Yuan.

Despite controversies over his life and career, his position as a master calligrapher and painter is unquestioned. His paintings were famous in four aspects, namely calligraphy, painting, poetry and seal. His achievements were well-known and well-documented. His works were sought after by Japanese and Indian collectors, so he is a forerunner of international cultural exchanges in Beijing.

As a master artist during a transitional period, Zhao Mengfu advocated what he called "ancient taste" and proposed a natural and plain style, reversing the artistic trend that emphasised neatness and attention to detail, which had been dominant since the Northern Song Dynasty. He put emphasis on painting and sketching from nature, rather than copying. He believed that calligraphy and painting shared the same origin, so he tried to integrate both by incorporating calligraphy into painting and using painting to express emotions. Among the numerous artists dwelling in Dadu at the time, Zhao Mengfu was skilled in all kinds of painting genres, such as portraits, landscape, flowers, birds and beasts. He was also an innovative artist. He is highly appraised in the history of painting in China. During the Mongol rule of China, he rejuvenated the traditional Chinese painting by incorporating Mongolian styles and Chinese styles, thus initiating a new style with lasting influences.

With the decline of the Yuan Dynasty, the style initiated by Zhao Mengfu and his contemporary artists was carried forward by artists from the Yangtze River delta, notably "the Four Masters of the Yuan Dynasty," Huang Gongwang, who was famous for "Dwelling in Fuchun Mountains," Wang Meng, Wu Zhen and Ni Zan. The distinctive features of their paintings inspired countless artists of later generations.

Transition from Yuan Style to Qing Style

Emperors Taizu (1328–1398) and Yongle (1360–1424) were both patrons of literati painting. Although both of them established their rule by force, they appreciated the nee for the protection and development of traditional Chinese art. As a dynasty established by the Chinese after Jin and Yuan, two dynasties established by minorities, Ming rulers and artists embraced the golden era for Chinese painting.

Each and every dynasty in Chinese history has its rise and fall, and the Ming Dynasty (1368–1644) is no exception. Painting in the Ming Dynasty also followed the path of rise and fall.

Although the Ming Dynasty did not have any imperial art academies like those of the Song, the Ming Dynasty did appoint many court painters, which gave rise to a golden time of palace painting and made Beijing the centre of painting in China. Painters came to Beijing from all around the country, which stimulated the integration of various styles into a brand-new one.

Some painters in the early Ming Dynasty were good at painting landscape and bamboo, but they served as government officials in the court because they excelled in calligraphy. Their paintings blended the style of scholarly painting with palace painting. The most prominent figure in this period was Wang Fu, whose masterpiece was "The Eight Scenes of Beijing." As a great calligrapher, he was appointed to work in Wenyuange (Pavilion of Literary Profundity) in 1430 and remained there until his death. "The Eight Scenes of Beijing," which is now kept in National Museum of China, was painted while he was accompanying the emperor on tours around Beijing in 1413 and 1414. It is the earliest and the most important painting of the sceneries of Beijing. The wash painting depicts the famous eight scenes of Beijing, namely Sunset at Jintai, Ripples of Taiye, Spring Shade of Jade Islet, Rainbow at Yuquan, Greenery at Juyong, Trees at Jimen, Morning Moon over Marco Polo Bridge and Sunshine on Snow at the Western Hills. "The eight scenes in the painting are of various kinds and are painted delicately. It was in the typical style of Wang Fu, with traces of mountain and water paintings from the Song and Yuan dynasties." Wang Fu was famous for his paintings of bamboo. "His style is a blending of masculine strength and feminine softness." He was honoured as the top painter of China at the time and represented the top level of art in Beijing.

The Ming Dynasty was a golden time for Chinese painting, with numerous painters, various styles and schools emerging. Traditional genres such as figures, mountains and waters, flowers and birds flourished while scholarly paintings such as plums, orchids and bamboo were well-developed. The artistic achievements of Beijing also led to the development of folklore paintings and frescoes.

Heavy colour figure painting emerged in the Ming Dynasty. Frescoes of the same style and technique remain today, such as those in Fahai Temple in Beijing. Located at the southern foot of Cuiwei Mountain in the west of Beijing, the temple was built between 1436 and 1449 with funds raised by Li Tong, a eunuch during the reign of Ming Emperor Zhengtong (1427–64). The fresco "Lord Brahma," inside the main hall, was painted by a group of artists from the Ministry of Works, including Wuan Fuqing, Wang Shu, Zhang Ping, Wang Yi, Gu Xing, Li Yuan, Pan Fu and Xu Fulin. The painting depicts the various gods with Brahma at the centre; they were all painted vividly and in complicated layouts. The elaborate style, which can be traced back to the Tang and Song dynasties, demonstrates the transition from Tang and Song Buddhist frescoes to Ming style palace painting.

Liberal political environment, stable social and economic development lead to innovations in art. In the latter half of the Ming Dynasty, the most significant development was the introduction of western art into China.

The two most prominent figures in this period were Matteo Ricci and Johann Adam Schall, two European missionaries who introduced western elements to Chinese painting. They both presented to the emperors western paintings of icons. In 1600, Matteo Ricci (1552–1610), a Catholic Jesuit missionary from Italy, came to Beijing to present an ancient and a contemporary catholic icon to Emperor Wanli (1563–1620). After obtaining permission to stay in Beijing, he presented the emperor with another three western paintings of the royal palace of Spain, St. Mark's Cathedral of Rome and Venice Square. Those were the first western paintings introduced to China. The icon was hung in the Xuanwumen Catholic

Church. According to accounts by witnesses, the portrait of Madonna looked vivid, as if she was looking across the cathedral. That visual effect of western painting stirred the interest of Ming artists. When asked by those artists, Matteo answered, "In Chinese painting, only the light is depicted, so the figures are flat, whereas in western painting, both the light and the shade are depicted, so the figures are three-dimensional." He also introduced western engravings into China. After him, Johann Adam Schall, a missionary from Prussia, came to Beijing with paintings "Jesus Returning to Jerusalem," "Crucifixion of Jesus" and "Jesus on the Cross." Through churches and albums, those western paintings had a profound impact on Chinese painting throughout the Ming and Qing dynasties.

Collective Wisdom for Imperial Relics and Empire's Resurgence

The emergence of the Qing Dynasty (1644–1911) didn't change Beijing's position as the national political and cultural centre. From the Qing army's march into the Shanhai Pass, enthronement of Emperor Shunzhi (1638–61) who selected Beijing as the capital, to the abdication of Puyi (1906–1967), the last emperor, Beijing remained as the centre of mainstream painting while demonstrating the features of carrying forward ancient tradition, valuing tradition yet remaining all-embracing, open and inclusive. As the Manchu people became the new rulers of the Central Plain, they gave rise to a host of painters of imperial clans and Manchu painters. The development of painting in the Qing Dynasty feature diverse schools, popular Western style and the emergence of one talented artist after another.

Unlike in the previous dynasties, a journalistic and even "politics-assisting" function was added to the palace paintings of the Qing Dynasty on top of the elegant taste of scholars. "Politics-assisting" could be understood as artistic creations that depict the emperor's activities or major political events in an organised and well-planned manner. A typical example is the painting titled "Southern Tour of Emperor Kangxi." To consolidate his rule, Emperor Kangxi (1654–1722) made six inspection tours to the south during his reign. There are many stories circulating among the ordinary people concerning the visits of Emperor Kangxi and his grandson, Emperor Qianlong (1711–99) to the regions south of the Yangtze River. However, "Southern Tour of Emperor

Kangxi" gives a relatively reliable itinerary of Emperor Kangxi. According to historical data, after the first southern tour, Emperor Kangxi had recruited painters to describe his second tour in 1691 throughout the whole journey. For that matter, the Qing Court recruited professional painter Wang Hui as the chief court painter in Beijing who led other court painters in creating 12 volumes in six years. The 12 volumes are well-linked yet independent, describing the second southern tour of Emperor Kangxi, towns and villages, famous scenic spots, local conditions and customs along the journey in a detailed fashion. Given the grand scene and numerous figures, they are considered to be among the greatest works of reportage painting ever. Born to a family of artists, Wang Hui enjoyed the title of "Painting Sage" at that time. He came to Beijing aged 60 to lead the creation of the southern tour and lived in Beijing for eight years, exerting a huge impact on the painting landscape in Beijing. Now, Painting of "Southern Tour of Emperor Kangxi" is regarded as a priceless treasure. But only Volumes 1, 9, 10, 11 and 12 are kept in the Palace Museum in Beijing and other volumes are scattered in museums or private collections in the United States, France and Canada. That said, we can still witness the superb artistry of court painters and the strong "publicity" function of journalistic painting of the Qing Dynasty from the five volumes collected in the Palace Museum.

The Qing Dynasty had a grand team of court painters, with numerous well-known painters, and a good many of works of different periods of the Qing Dynasty have been handed down. Apart from the professional painters given the responsibility of recording actual events and "assisting politics," some painters "serving the court" are "official painters" who were also fine poets and calligraphers. While inheriting the painting traditions of past dynasties, they were knowledgeable and well-informed of the latest painting skills and artistic concepts and put them into practice in their artistic innovations. The fact that western missionary painters were employed as court painters since Emperor Kangxi serves as proof that the Qing Dynasty adopted an open attitude toward different schools of art.

The western influence brought by western painters to Beijing's painting scene could be traced back to the late-Ming Dynasty. Matteo Ricci, who received courteous reception in the imperial court and Johann Adam Schall, who witnessed the dynastic change from Ming to Qing, presented western paintings to the emperor to smooth their way for propagating religion in China. In the Qing Dynasty, from Emperor Kangxi to Emperor Qianlong, western missionaries with artistic talents were recruited as court painters. The most well-known foreign painters who made a living and sought honour by painting in the imperial court included Giuseppe Castiglione, Ignaz Sichelbarth, Joannes Damascenus Salusti and Jean Denis Attiret. Among them, Giuseppe Castiglione was the most influential with the largest number of works handed down to this day. Until now, works of Giuseppe Castiglione on the auction have never failed to attract widespread attention. "Ping Ye Ming Qiu," produced by Giuseppe Castiglione, sold at auction for HK$17.645 million (US$1.9 million) at Christie's spring auction in 2000; and in Christie's autumn auction the same year, his work "Deers in an Autumn Forest" sold for HK$8.845 million (US$1.4 million).

Giuseppe Castiglione, a 19-year-old Italian missionary, came to China in 1715 and was employed as a court painter by Emperor Kangxi, the beginning of a career that lasted more than 50 years. As he brought in western painting skills and demonstrated the charm of light and shade painting of Europe to the emperor and other court painters, he was successively put in important positions by Emperor Kangxi and his successors. As a versatile artist skilled in all painting genres, Castiglione became a representative person of court painting under the reign of Emperor Yongzheng (1678–1735) and Emperor Qianlong. He integrated Chinese and western skills in painting to create precise and vivid effect, forming a new painting style. He also knew fully the "Art of Living" at Chinese court and strictly abided by the rules on the court painters of the Qing Dynasty. He would draw up a sketch and presented it to the emperor for approval before starting painting. As a result, his innovations were achieved in a moderate and gradual way and European painting skills were gradually passed on to Chinese court painters, rendering the palace paintings of the Qing Dynasty with of a combination of Chinese and western styles, showing a unique style that is different from court paintings of previous dynasties.

Painting for the ordinary people also prospered toward the end of the Qing Dynasty. Scroll paintings, and paintings on lanterns and fans depicting subject matters familiar to the people became very popular among the general public. Themes of the folk paintings mainly cover popular fiction and stories of operas. Characters from popular stories such as *Xi You Ji* (*Journey to the West*) and *Jin Gu Qiguan* (*Modern and Ancient Wonders*) were well received. Painting stores at Longfusi and Liulichang—bustling streets of Beijing at that time—were doing very good business.

One should not overlook the development of art theories as part of the development of painting in the Qing Dynasty. Many theoretical works were produced by both artists and theoreticians during this period.

How many artists who thrived in Beijing have yet to be discovered? And how many works representing the charm of different periods of painting history of China and continuing the artistic lineage of Beijing have yet to be unearthed?

Beijing is home to the Forbidden City, which is China's largest museum of ancient culture and art. In this museum one can find a treasure of paintings created throughout the city's history. It houses more than 130 paintings on thin silks of the Yuan Dynasty, masterpieces of well-known painters of the Ming Dynasty including the Wumen Painting School, palace paintings and masterpieces of western painters serving in the imperial court of the Qing Dynasty. If you would like to have a look at the most splendid, flourishing, innovative classic paintings typical of China in the history of Chinese art, Beijing is the place to be.

Poetry as a Recorder of History

Chinese characters and poetry are magical. Foreign scholars committed to sinology often give themselves Chinese names. They select characters from Chinese scriptures and poems that are homophonic to their names but which also demonstrate their ambitions. Shi Jingqian (Jonathan D. Spence), Kong Lifei (Alden Kuhn) and Fei Zhengqing (John King Fairbank) are examples. As a result, both their names and works are familiar to Chinese readers.

It is not known how many people today read ancient Chinese poetry and scriptures. However, even youths are familiar with overseas films such as *Yishu Lihua Ya Haitang (Pear Blossoms over Chinese Crab Apples, Lolita), Hunduan Lanqiao (Sorrows over the Blue Bridge, Waterloo Bridge)* and *Ciqing Ke Wentian (Eternal Love, Howards End)*. The original English names of these films do not mean anything to the Chinese. However, their translation into Chinese-style names can stir the enthusiasm and imagination of the Chinese to discover *Lolita,* a story about the relationship between a teenage girl and a middle-aged man, *Waterloo Bridge,* a sad love story that took place on this famous bridge, and that *Howards End,* a story of lingering love.

The strength of Chinese culture and the charm of Chinese poetry are evidenced by the above two examples of West meets East. The history of Chinese literature, poetry in particular, is like a river of pearls and jewels, and Beijing has long been a creative force associated with this literary river.

Riches from Poets Born in Hard Times

The history of Beijing as a capital began in 1153 when Wanyan Liang, Emperor Hailingwang, of the Jin Dynasty (1115 – 1234), became the first emperor to rule from the city. Since then, Beijing has been a capital city for about 860 years and the nation's capital for much of that time. Despite having taken the throne through trickery and purges, Wanyan Liang was a great poet who admired Chinese culture.

Accomplished emperors were also usually diligent scholars. In his childhood, Wanyan Liang placed literary studies ahead of military training among his interests. According to historical records, he enjoyed writing calligraphy on Chinese fans when he was still a vassal prince.

He wrote, "If I held supreme power, I would usher in a time of peace and order in the country," a line demonstrating his ambition. When he became the emperor of Jin Dynasty, he aspired to build a capital city unlike any other. His poems were grand and powerful. He once led his army to Weiyang (central and northern parts of today's Yangzhou) to realize his ambition for territorial expansion. "The gauges of carts and scripts shall be unified across tens of thousands of miles; so why should [lands] south of the Yangtze River be allowed to remain outside? I will order a million troops to conquer the West Lake area, and I will ride a horse up to the highest peak of Wu Mountain."

Traditionally, most poets in China specialised in writing *shi* (poems) or *ci* (a type of classical Chinese poetry), the two main genres of Chinese poetry. However, Wanyan Liang was an exception. He was adept at both. According to historical records, he wrote a *ci* entitled *Xiqianying* when he despatched an expedition army to the south. It was full of allusions to Chinese culture and illustrated the emperor's literary achievement.

Wanyan Liang ultimately failed to realise his lifelong ambitions and died in misery when he led an expedition across the Yangtze River at Guazhou into the Southern Song Dynasty's (1127–79) territory in September 1161. There, aged 40, one of his generals, Wanyan Yuanyi, assassinated him by strangling him. In April 1162, he was demoted, posthumously, to the title of King Hailing. In January 1181, Wanyan Liang was again demoted to the level of a commoner. Although he established the central capital of the Jin Dynasty, he failed to go down in history as an authentic emperor. However, his excellent poems have remained for posterity.

After Wanyan Liang, poetry

took root and flourished in the imperial house of the Jin Dynasty, perhaps more than during any other dynasty. The works of Emperors Shizong (reign: 1161–89) and Zhangzong (reign: 1189–1208) were closer to the authentic Chinese culture in terms of Confucianism and psychological aesthetics. But the Jin Dynasty's life was brief, and it went into decline in the face of Mongol invasions during its final years. However, these hard times fostered many patriotic poems. Yuan Haowen (1190–1257) is representative of that time.

Yuan Haowen was of the House of Tuoba of the Xianbei nationality during the Northern Wei Dynasty (AD 386–557). At 32, he became an official, serving first as the magistrate of Nanyang County and then as a minister in various departments. The Mongols detained him in Liaocheng City after the Jin Dynasty's fall. Upon being released, he returned home to live as a poet. He was the most important and prolific Jin poet, and 1,400 of his poems still exist today.

The life of Yuan Haowen strengthens the notion that the achievements of poets spring from the nation's misfortunes. Living through the decline and fall of his country, Yuan's poems recorded his time's historic events. In them, he lamented the fall of his rulers and the sufferings of the people while expansively expressing his ambitions. When the Mongols besieged Bianjing (today's Kaifeng), he wrote a poem lamenting the fall of the then capital that became famous. Yuan Haowen was adept at various genres of poetry, including *ci;* we can still read 300 of his *ci* today.

Yuan Haowen made another major contribution to posterity: the preservation of the litterateurs of the Jin and Yuan (1271–1368) dynasties. He compiled the ten-volume *Zhongzhou Collection,* with the one-volume *Zhongzhou Poetry* as an appendix. This huge book includes 2,026 poems by 251 poets of the Jin Dynasty. Each of the poets is introduced by a short biography or a comment on their poems. Yuan Haowen's aim was to record history through poetry. The book is now regarded as an important source in Jin Dynasty research.

Poetry Developing Abreast with Society

People who read the line "the great man, Genghis Khan, only knew how to shoot eagles with an arrow" may wonder whether a nomadic people could excel in literature. Following this logic, they believe that Kublai Khan must have been illiterate. However, he wrote the first poem in *The Complete Collection of Yuan Poems.*

Kublai Khan developed Beijing as his golden capital, a city admired around the world. His poem, especially the last line, was unparalleled at the time in terms of perspective and ambition.

Like emperors of the Jin Dynasty, all Yuan Dynasty emperors were great admirers and students of Chinese culture. The integration and assimilation of various cultures laid a foundation for the development of literature during the Yuan Dynasty, in particular *yuanqu* (a type of verse popular in the Yuan Dynasty) and *zaju* (poetic drama), popular genres comparable to the famous poetry of the Tang (618–907) and Song dynasties. Many excellent poets from minority ethnic groups left numerous masterpieces for posterity.

In the century from 1271, when Kublai Khan established the Yuan Dynasty, to 1368, when Zhu Yuanzhang established the Ming Dynasty in Yingtian (today's Nanjing), there were two famous minority poets. The first was Yelu Chucai (1190–1244), a Khitan nobleman who was discovered by Genghis Khan and later elevated to the peak of his political career during Kublai Khan's reign. The second was Sadula (1272–1355), a famous painter and poet of the late-Yuan Dynasty.

In 1215, Genghis Khan took Yanjing (today's Beijing) by force. When he heard that Yelu Chucai was a great political talent, he consulted him. Having lost confidence in the Jin Dynasty, Yelu Chucai decided to serve in the court of Genghis Khan, and went on to exert a profound influence on Genghis and his descendents. His measures laid the foundations for the establishment of the Yuan Dynasty.

Yelu Chucai was an outstanding politician. He was born into the imperial house of Khitan and grew up in Yanjing. Apart from his political achievements, he made enormous contributions to the development of culture. He is the Chinese who proposed the concept of longitude. He compiled and revised a couple of calendar books. He used to follow Genghis Khan and Ogedei Khan in their expeditions and wrote many poems, 660 of which were collected in a book. He was familiar with the scenery and customs of the frontiers, and described them in his poems. He wrote 50 poems about the western regions of China, which became important resources for historians. Yelu Chucai wrote well in different genres of poetry. His poems were grand in style and expressed his feelings about the changing political climate. As a descendant of Khitan, he attached great importance to the preservation of Khitan culture. *The Song of Inebriation,* the longest existing poem written in the Khitan language, was translated by him into Chinese and put into his collection of poems.

Yelu Chucai served for 30 years in the court of Genghis Khan and Ogedei, until his death on May 14, 1244. When he died, the nation was grief-stricken. Officials, especially those from the Chinese nation, mourned this accomplished politician. In 1261, Kublai Khan followed Yelu's will and moved his remains back to his home, Wong Hill, to the east of Yuquan Hill in the Summer Palace. Yelu Chucai was a great politician, and also a titan of literature.

Sadula was another Yuan Dynasty artist, equal in stature to Yelu Chucai. He was a poet, painter and calligrapher. His ancestors came from western China. He was born in Yanmen (today's Dai County in Shanxi Province), so he was dubbed "the genius of Yanmen." Sadula left 800 poems, which are included in *The Collection of Yanmen.* In them he described scenery, recorded events in the palace, depicted people's lives and commented on social injustice. In *The New History of the Yuan Dynasty,* his poems were described as "unparalleled during his time."

Sadula was a great thinker who held strong views on life and society and expressed them in his poems. As an upright official, he often wrote poems for his colleagues who were equally upright. In the mid- and late-Yuan Dynasty, there were constant peasant uprisings. Inspired by seeing these scenes of conflict, he wrote poems to express his opposition to war and his wish for peace.

From his poems, it can be seen clearly that he followed the literary styles of the Wei (AD 220–265), Jin (AD 265–420) and Tang dynasties. His poems described the realities of life and expressed strong emotions. Yu Ji, another poet of the Yuan Dynasty, praised Sadula's poems. Yang Weizhen, a contemporary of Sadula, thought his poems set the standard for the Yuan Dynasty. Zhang Peiheng, a contemporary scholar, wrote in an essay on Yuan poetry, "The last and the highest stage of poetry of the Yuan Dynasty were marked by two outstanding poets, Sadula and Yang Weizhen." It can be concluded that Sadula elevated Yuan poetry to a towering height.

High-Ranking Officials with Poetic Talent

Because of the nature of the imperial examination system and an official's education, many, if not most, Ming Dynasty (1368–1644) officials had a refined aesthetic sense. Especially during retirement, their pursuit of traditional Chinese arts such as calligraphy, ink-wash painting, composing and playing music and writing was prized and respected as such.

According to scholars of Chinese literature, the Ming Dynasty novel was the best example of that art form. Though classical poetry was past its most glorious age by the advent of the Ming, there were always poets who worked hard to bring innovations to that great tradition and who crafted many highly regarded classical poems.

In its 300-year history, the Ming Dynasty produced more great poets than any other dynasty. Their poetry took many twists and turns. In the Emperor Hongwu (1368–98) and Jianwen (1399–1402) years, most of the poets followed the Tang writers' tendency to "express their experience." During the Emperor Yongle (1403–24) and Tianshun (1457–64) periods, the gorgeous style that was produced by some prestigious ministers and that focused on social life, dominated the era. Later, in the Emperor Jiajing (1521–66) and Longqing (1567–72) years, most poets returned to imitating the ancients. The poetry of this time resembled more works from the Wei (AD 220–265) and Jin (AD 265–420) dynasties. Later, some insightful poets argued that a poem should come from the poets themselves rather than what others have said. Poetry that had long been in the shadow of the ancients achieved a breakthrough. Poems in this period were again full of militancy and observations of social and political reality.

In the first lunar month of 1421, the 19th year of Emperor Yongle's reign, the Ming government officially moved its capital to Beijing. Of the many remarkable poets of the Ming Dynasty, Liu Ji and Yu Qian were the best known and had the deepest relationships with Beijing.

Liu Ji, an excellent strategist, politician, writer and thinker, was affectionately called Liu Bowen by his peers. To this day Beijing's children read stories and recite nursery rhymes about the legend of Liu building the city. Actually, Liu Ji, historically speaking, had no connection with the building of Beijing. He died in 1375, 46 years before Emperor Yongle moved the capital to Beijing.

Still, Liu Ji is a great figure in Beijingers' hearts and minds, but even without those legends he fully deserves the title of master poet. He is considered one of the three masters of poetry and prose in the early Ming Dynasty; the other two are Song Lian and Gao Qi. Educator Cai Yuanpei praised Liu as "the most successful character of the Ming Dynasty." Japanese scholar Junichi Okuno described him as "riding on the crest of success, pacifying the whole country, opening up a new world and expounding in writing. It seems only Liu Ji could do all of these." People loved him because of his concern for the fate of the state and the welfare of the people, about which he wrote numerous works, including *Ciyun*. One verse asks: "Since thousands of horses and soldiers ran amok on the Central Plains, how many states along the Yangtze River and the Huai River have survived?" When he saw thousands of poor villages, he wrote in *Rain and Snow*, "Why are the innocent common people suffering in the wild?" In *A Peasant Family*, he wrote: "The government should cherish the land tax that peasants earned with hard work."

Liu Ji left more than 220 essays, 1,301 poems and 221 works of *ci* (a type of classical Chinese poetry). In *The History of the Ming*, it says: "His essays are imposing and full of newness, making him the grand master of a generation." An expert on the Ming Dynasty, Shen Deqian, described Liu's poetry in his *Analytic Essays on Ming Poetry* as "unique, transcendent and definitely masterpieces." *The Siku Quanshu (Complete Library in the Four Branches of Literature)* created by the Qing government noted: "His poetry is restrained and dignified, unique in its style and good enough to rival Gao Qi."

Yu Qian was the only Ming poet whose individual fate and political career were closely tied to Beijing. He wrote *Song to the Lime*, including the lines "None since the advent of time have escaped death, may my loyalty forever illuminate the annals of history."

Yu Qian (1398–1457) was an honest and upright official and a war hero who had provided disaster relief to the people and was subsequently held in esteem by them before he was ultimately betrayed, slandered and murdered.

During the reign of Emperor Zhengtong (1435–49), the Oirat Mongols invaded and captured the emperor. Yu Qian proposed a new emperor, Emperor Jingtai, and personally led the army to guard the capital, finally repelling the enemy. The victory proved what a great general and a courageous national hero Yu Qian was. His army defeated the enemy in only five days. He had improved the fighting capacity of the capital's army and formed it into a powerful mobile force. The Oirats never dared covet Beijing again. More importantly, this victory promoted frontier construction, the recapture of many fortresses and key towns and lengthened the reign of the Ming Dynasty.

The battle not only put Yu Qian on the scroll of the history, but also led to misery in his later life. Former Emperor Zhengtong was eventually released by the Oirats, and launched a coup with the support of eunuchs and courtiers, in the first lunar month of Jingtai's eighth year on the throne (1457). Emperor Zhengtong abolished Jingtai's reign and re-ascended the throne. Believing the slanders of some politicians, Zhengtong had Yu Qian killed, prompting widespread regret. His body was quietly laid in a coffin by an official named Chen Kui, and was carried back to his homeland, Hangzhou, by his son-in-law. He was buried on the shores of West Lake where another famous general, Yue Fei, had been buried. To recall the integrity and imperishable achievements of the two heroes, later generations developed a verse, saying, "Only with Yu and Yue as guards, can people enjoy the beauty of West Lake."

Liu Ji and Yu Qian, whether in legend or in reality, remain giants in the world of Chinese classical poetry, and also in the history of Beijing and its people.

Inspired by Beautiful Scenery

After the rejuvenation of poetry in the late Ming Dynasty (1368–1644) and its subsequent decline, the Qing Dynasty brought another high point. Many poems written during the Qing Dynasty reflected social contradictions and realities. Qing poets experimented with style and expression enriching poetic development. By critically learning from poets of previous dynasties, in particular the Tang (AD 618–907) and Song (AD 960–1229), the Qing poets' achievements, styles and genres surpassed those of the Yuan (1271–1368) and Ming dynasties, preparing the way for modern Chinese poetry.

Qing greats included Gu Yanwu, Wang Fuzhi, Huang Zongxi, Qian Qianyi and Wu Weiye of the early Qing; Shen Deqian, Zheng Banqiao, Zhang Wentao, Yuan Mei, Jiang Shiquan and Zhao Yi of the mid-Qing; and Gong Zizhen, Wei Yuan, Huang Zunxian, Kang Youwei, Liang Qichao and Tan Sitong of the late-Qing.

Among the prominent Qing poets were two native masters in Beijing: Emperor Qianlong (reign: 1735–96) and Nalan Xingde, a Manchurian nobleman.

Emperor Qianlong was not thought of as a poet in the history of Chinese literature, but he was its most prolific poet. He wrote more than 43,000 poems, nearly as many as the 50,000 poems written during the entire 290-year Tang Dynasty. Liang Shizheng, a Qing scholar, praised the emperor for his diligence in study. Emperor Qianlong grew up studying the Confucian culture, poetry, calligraphy and painting. As a learned man, he was also an accomplished and wise monarch, second only to his grandfather, Emperor Kangxi (reign: 1661–1722), in historical standing. He was moved to write poems regardless where he was, and this dedication built his fame as a poet.

Emperor Qianlong wrote many poems about Beijing. Apart from imperial sites such as the Forbidden Palace and the Summer Palace, Emperor Qianlong wrote poems even for small villages he visited. However, as he was an emperor with an unpredictable nature, few of his poems are familiar to people today. He liked to use rare characters and expressions in his poems and strictly followed the rules and forms of classical poetic composition; so his poems are generally regarded as flashy and without substance. Therefore, some of excellent poems he wrote have been overlooked.

In the history of Chinese poetry, there have been various styles, such as restrained and unconstrained, but one style created during the Qing Dynasty was named for the poet who created it rather than its structure. Nalan Style was named after Nalan Xingde.

Nalan Xingde came from a noble family. His father was Mingzhu, a minister during the reign of Emperor Kangxi. His mother was the fifth daughter of Prince Ajige. His family belonged to the Yellow Banner and was one of the top eight Manchurian households in the early Qing Dynasty. He was a prodigy as a child. At 17, he entered the Imperial College to study. At 19, he presided over the compilation of *Tongzhitang (Annotations of Scriptures)*, a 1,792-volume Confucian collection. Later, he established himself as an erudite historian and writer. In 1674, he married a woman named Lu, who died giving birth two years later. Bereavement inspired his book-length lamentation *Drinking Water*. Wang Guowei, a modern scholar, praised him highly: "Nalan followed a natural approach in his artistic observation and creation, because he was able to retain his nature, which had not been contaminated. He was the only naturalistic poet since the end of Northern Song Dynasty." Kuang Zhouyi, a late Qing poet, honoured Nalan as "the top early Qing poet."

Today, the line "If time had stopped when we first met…" is popular among young people, but few know it was written by Nalan Xingde. "If time had stopped when we first met, why would we paint the sad autumn wind on a fan? Easily we changed our love for our beloved, but we regard our beloved as changeable." This philosophic poem demonstrated the naturalism to which Nalan Xingde was dedicated. At the age of 22, he was appointed a third-level courtier by Emperor Kangxi and was soon elevated to the first level. As a handsome warrior, he followed the emperor on his expeditions and tours across the country. Although he was a young courtier with a bright future, he was by no means a social climber and hated the life of an official. Living in luxurious mansions and working in grand palaces, he longed for life in the countryside. At 24, he collected his poems in a volume titled *Cemao Anthology* and wrote *Drinking Water*. The two books were later combined into *The Collection of Poems* by Nalan, which consists of 349 poems. This book was popular at the time and was highly praised by scholars.

Nalan Xingde was active in promoting cultural development. He had many friends and he was eager to help them with their difficulties. Lushui Pavilion (today's Enbo Pavilion in the former residence of Soong Ch'ing-ling in Beijing), his home, was a famous meeting place for scholars, who gathered there to exchange views on culture. These meetings promoted the cultural prosperity that endured during the period from Emperor Kangxi to Emperor Qianlong.

In 1685, Nalan Xingde died at the young age of 31. His life and poems have exerted a profound influence on later literature and culture. In *Chunming Unofficial History,* Zhang Henshui, a novelist of the Republic of China era, wrote about a prodigy who died at 30. Zhang lamented his friend's death with the line, "Reading his poems, I knew that he would have an early death, just like Nalan." Nalan wrote a number of poems about the scenery in the Western Hills of Beijing where he accompanied the emperor. Those poems have been eternalised along with the scenery in Beijing's long history.

Holderlin, a classical German poet, wrote a popular line, "Man. Live poetically!" Heidegger, a German philosopher, explained the line this way, "If we call this multi-aspect space the world, then the world is the place inhabited by people…."

For people in Beijing, this city, with its 860 years of history as a capital in China and an even longer history of poetry, is a place to inhabit poetically; and with its magnificent cultural treasures, it is truly a poetic home.

Legendary Chinese Costume

At the Summer Palace in April 1983, a young girl was led by her mother to the foot of a magnolia tree in glorious bloom to have her photo taken. But she didn't want the same kind of bland photo that most people took in front of the tree. Not far away, she noticed a small pavilion with a sign that read, "Women's dress of the Manchu nationality." She ran to it, wondering how much it would cost for a picture of her dressed in a *qizhuang,* a kind of traditional dress worn by ladies of the Manchu court. However, as she drew near, she was disappointed to find the dress was just paperboard; vivid but not real. It seemed that by standing behind it and placing one's face between the collar and the headwear, anyone could get a picture of themselves looking as though they were wearing a real red *qizhuang,* just like one worn by the young Empress Dowager Cixi (regency: 1861–1908).

At the beginning of April 1989, she was back at the same part of the Summer Palace. This time, she found a real *qizhuang;* it was a prop for souvenir pictures. The red gown had worn thin, and the huge peony on the headwear seemed to be wilting, but this did not curb her enthusiasm to put on the beautiful gown and have her picture taken. Today, 24 years later, this picture is still well-preserved because it holds sentimental value.

Various Chinese costumes are popular and receive great exposure; movie stars appear in blue and white porcelain-like dresses or silk-embroidered "imperial robes" on the red carpet of the Cannes Film Festival; foreigners who come to learn crosstalk and Beijing opera often dress in Tang suits to show their admiration for Chinese culture. On special occasions, the girl and her peers in Beijing take from the bottom of their wardrobes a gorgeous Chinese dress that has been carefully stored in a box with mothballs, with knotted buttons, sequins and beautiful embroidery. Some people have a real silk or satin gown, others are made from linen, but they are usually a classic, elegant and valuable Chinese outfit handcrafted by the Ruifuxiang Silk Store.

The subtle details, the intertwining silk threads, the exquisite button loops, and the little embroidered flowers all contribute to a gorgeous Chinese costume that is the pride of this ancient city and its people.

Clothing Embroidered with Pearls, Gold and Rhinoceros Horn

The people of the Nüzhen nationality in the Jin Dynasty (1115–1234) did not leave many cultural relics of costumes, partly because of their custom of cremating their dead. The few graves of the Jin Dynasty that have been unearthed in Beijing, Liaoning Province, Inner Mongolia, Heilongjiang Province and elsewhere all show traces of burning. But records in *The History of the Great Kingdom of Jin* and *History of Clothing in Jin Dynasty* are fascinating to later generations, because they show that these people valued fine clothing.

Before Emperor Taizu (reign: 1115–23) founded the Jin Dynasty, the Nüzhen people were affiliated with the State of Liao. After the Jin Dynasty was founded, the Nüzhen moved toward the territory of the State of Yan. They found the Liao's higher level of development was also reflected in its costumes and etiquette system, and so they learned from the Liao. Two administrative systems came into being; one in the north and one in the south. As the Nüzhen approached the Yellow River basin, they encountered the elegant and highly complex dress code of the Song Dynasty (960–1279). As they continued learning, they developed their own imperial robe, the *tongtian guan* (a kind of tall crown), and *jiangsha pao* (a type of crimson robe).

From then on, a range of dress requirements according to rank and position were introduced. A prince would wear a *yuanyou* crown when travelling, and the officials had a dress code that was almost as complicated as that of the Song system. Detailed provisions were made even in terms of the colours they could wear. For example, round-collared robes, which were the court dress, were purple for fifth rank officials, red for sixth and seventh rank officials and green for officials of the eighth and ninth ranks. To differentiate themselves from the guards, civil officials carried gold and silver-coloured bags decorated with images of fish.

After Zhongdu (present day Beijing) was established as the Jin capital, the robes of officials of the Jin Dynasty became increasingly splendid, and were embroidered with gold ornaments on the chest, shoulders and sleeves. In the Jin Shizong period, the size of embroideries was closely related to the ranking of an official; the lower the rank, the smaller the embroidery. For example, the size was 15 centimetres (cm) for officials above third rank, and 9 cm for officials above sixth rank. A minor official was allowed no embroidery at all, and could only wear robes made of *zhimaluo,* an inexpensive clothing material.

Though the Jin people were inspired by the local Han costumes, they were proud of their origins, and this was reflected in their clothing. The robes of the Jin Dynasty were classified by season. Normally, the spring robe was embroidered with images of birds and flowers; the autumn robe was embroidered with images of bears, deer or forest. The robes of officials were embroidered with jade, gold and rhinoceros horn; the materials used reflected their rankings.

Jin people liked to wear fur. According to *The History of the Great Kingdom of Jin,* "In the barren land, only fur could resist cold. Therefore, all people, whether they were rich or poor, made clothes out of furs. The rich usually wore clothes made from flax and brocade in spring and summer. They occasionally used fine fur and cloth. In autumn and winter, they wore clothes made from the furs of martens, foxes or lambs. The poor wore the same clothes in spring and autumn. In winter, they wore clothes made from the skins of oxen, horses, pigs, sheep, cats, dogs, bears, snakes, wild dogs or deer."

Women in the Jin Dynasty typically wore a lower garment called an "apron skirt." In *History of Clothing in Jin Dynasty,* there are records showing the Nüzhen women favoured black or purple six-pleat apron skirts covered with embroidered flowers. A Jin girl wearing such a skirt, with red and green waistbands, would surely have looked charming, even before donning the shawls that indicated her social status.

Examples of Jin Dynasty costumes are exhibited in the Beijing Liao and Jin City Wall Museum. Many visitors to the museum find these costumes somehow familiar. The straight overlapping collars; the positioning of gusset and cincture on the left hand side of garments; as well as the slits designed for convenience when working, horse riding or shooting; and tight-fitting designs that were implemented to minimize the chances of snagging clothing; remained popular in North China, especially in Beijing, after the Jin Dynasty was overthrown. They were integrated into the costumes of the Han nationality, as well as those of the subsequent Mongol rulers.

Life is not Luxurious without Gold Thread

Farming culture, grassland culture, combined with European Christianity and West Asian Islamic cultures combined to produce a rich diversity of dress during the Yuan Dynasty (1271–1368).

Initially, the Mongolian nationality kept their dress style of "free-flowing hair with a cone-shaped bun, wearing cloth hats in winter and bamboo hats in summer." Fur hats, fur-lined jackets and leather boots made of marten and sheep pelts were the most common clothes. As one of the ethnic minority regimes in the history of China, the Yuan Dynasty divided people nationwide into four ranks. This differentiation in social status was also reflected in their dress. Typically, the Mongolian nobles were loudly dressed, the Semu (non-Han Chinese) people less so, while Han and southern Chinese dressed simply.

Long before the Mongols entered Shanhai Pass, the dress culture of the Han nationality had undergone change and development through a number of dynasties and influenced later generations. In the early stages of the Yuan Dynasty, the dress for Han memorial ceremonies had already been introduced, and the officials' costumes were divided into imperial dress, court dress and general dress.

Yuan officials wore plates to show their ranks. The top officials wore gold plates with a fighting tiger motif. Pure gold plates were second in order of rank, followed by silver plates. A person's social status was determined by the material of the plate worn at the waist.

Both silk weaving and embroidery techniques had reached a very high level in the Yuan Dynasty, which were reflected in the brilliant costumes, high-quality materials and attention to detail. Costumes of the Yuan Dynasty were adorned with gold-coloured thread, and gold-threaded textiles were very popular. According to historical data, the favourite dress material of people in the Yuan Dynasty was called *"nashishi,"* a golden Persian brocade.

Though there is some dispute as to whether Marco Polo really lived in the Chinese capital during the Yuan Dynasty, his description of the city's social life in *The Travels of Marco Polo,* to a considerable degree, complies with the description in *The History of the Yuan Dynasty* and other records. It records that the ruler of the Yuan Dynasty held 13 grand court meetings every year, and about 12,000 prominent officials and eminent people would attend.

The monarch and his subjects used golden cups to toast. Officials of high rank usually wore costumes made of colourful golden brocade, and the size of the flowers embroidered on the costumes indicated the ranks of such officials. What was most fascinating was undoubtedly the brilliant ornamental pearls, jade, gold thread and barbola on the emperor. According to Marco Polo's description, the emperor, while out hunting,

would sit in a big sedan chair, which was decorated with gold brocade, marten and ermine fur inside and covered with leopard fur outside. The sedan chair was carried by four elephants, and its "golden brilliance" was unparalleled.

In the Yuan Dynasty, the emperor and his civil and military officials wore *zhisunyi,* a kind of tight and short clothing, for grand banquets. *Zhisunyi* had a variety of styles for winter and summer and were worn with different combinations of accessories and

hats. Members of the imperial family usually wore hats inlaid with jewels. These jewels came from the contributions of each local government, as well as from the booty plundered on the course of territorial conquests in Europe and Asia.

The extravagant dress of Qing noblewomen can be seen in murals and paintings. They wore long gowns that reached the ground and a crown-shaped cap. They had to lean to one side and lower their heads when entering and leaving a yurt. The caps

were exquisitely decorated with red silk, gold brocade and blue velour, pheasant feathers, flowers and pearls.

The robes of the Mongolian noblewomen were big and loose. The sleeves wide with narrow openings. According to historical records of China's changing fashions during different dynasties, such robes were usually made with gold brocade, velour or wool, and featured strong, saturated colours, such as carmine, purple and gold. The Mongolian noblewomen regarded the gracefulness of the Han nationality as beauty. This reflected the integration of the dress cultures of the Mongol and Han nationalities, as well as the impact of Han style on the dress of the Mongols.

Diversification under Dress Code System

Zhu Yuanzhang, the founding emperor of the Ming Dynasty (1368–1644), was born into a poor family. It is said that before his military career he had lived a bitter life for many years. Different stories circulated among the people about him starving, begging and even becoming a monk so that he would be fed. His wife, who became Empress Xiao Cigao, was a frugal woman. Neither could tolerate spending money on fancy clothes, and they imposed strict bans on extravagance.

In 1368, the first year after the Ming Dynasty was founded, Zhu Yuanzhang promulgated an order prohibiting *hufu* (clothing of non-Han ethnic groups) and requiring clothes tailored in the style of the Tang Dynasty (AD 618–906) be worn again. He issued further regulations on the style, material and colour of the clothing worn by officials and civilians. The details include how literati and officials should tie their hair and wear black gauze caps. People from different classes and industries were required to wear different clothes. The rules stated, "Officials wear four-belted towels and robes with patterned round collars, and yellow or black mustn't be adopted; musicians wear green swastika towels on the head and red-green silk belts on the waist. Officials' wives wear gold-coated silver, and their rings must be gold balls, their bracelets silver, clothes plain and coats silk. Their maids wear double-horned caps and black mantles."

Two year laters, Zhu Yuanzhang issued detailed regulations on material and ornaments. Men and women had to dress plainly. There was to be "no silk or gold-wire embroidery or gauze on clothes, no gold, jade, pearls or silver on bracelets, and no patterns or gold-wire decorations on boots." Clear regulations were issued three years later on the colour of ordinary women's dresses. Purple was the only colour allowed for formal dresses, plain colours only for daily dresses and eye-catching colours favoured by dowagers, such as scarlet and yellow, were banned.

In 1380, *The Law of the Ming Dynasty* was issued. It stipulated that anyone who transgressed dress regulations would be punished. Officials would be caned 100 times and dismissed, while civilians would be caned 50 times and their relatives would also be punished. The offending clothes would be confiscated.

The dress code Zhu Yuanzhang developed was detailed, complete and unparalleled in history. It dictated the noble, simple dress style of the Ming Dynasty. We can see images of slender, handsome scholars and celebrities, and charming, virtuous women in numerous Ming Dynasty murals and paintings.

The dress code was strictly enforced. Despite this, Chinese costume culture saw a new high in the middle and late part of the Ming Dynasty. As the development of a social economy stimulated people's desire to dress individually, the entire clothing style transformed from plain to elaborate during the middle period of the Ming Dynasty. Throughout China's modern history it remained the model for the art of Chinese dress.

There were countless dress details developed during the Ming Dynasty, from caps, shoes to ornaments of different sizes. Several unique innovations are worth mentioning.

The first was the "melon rind cap." In the early days of the Ming Dynasty, a man usually wore a baggy green robe and a cap shaped like half a watermelon. The cap was made by sewing together six or eight pieces of cloth. This was what a fashionable man at that time would wear. It became even more popular during the Qing Dynasty.

Another was the mandarin square on official robes. Mandarin squares date to Wu Zetian's rule (AD655–683) in the Tang Dynasty. Later in the Yuan Dynasty, something called a "chest-and-back" appeared. This was a decorative animal pattern on the chest and back of garments. In the Ming Dynasty, the chest-and-back developed into a mandarin square sewn on the chest and back of an official robe. Different patterns on mandarin squares indicated different official ranks. Mandarin squares were in use by the Ming Dynasty. The dress code established by Zhu Yuanzhang did not overlook mandarin squares. They were covered by detailed regulations in the *Record of Regulations of the Ming Dynasty*, for example, kylin patterns could only be used on the mandarin squares of dukes and the emperor's sons-in-law; bird patterns on officials' mandarin squares indicated civil positions and animal patterns on military officers' robes signified power. There were specific regulations about what animals were to be embroidered on robes worn by officials and military officers of the nine ranks.

Women of the Ming Dynasty made significant contributions to the development of Chinese costume culture. They wore tight, long clothes. As one scholar wrote, "A skirt had six pleats which represent the six tributaries of the Xiangjiang River." By the end of the Ming Dynasty, a skirt had eight pleats and scores of folds around the waist, which, when the wearer was moving, looked just like ripples. Later in the Ming Dynasty, more decorations were added to skirts. A skirt had up to ten pleats around the waist, each a different colour. There was also a peacock tail skirt that was made of regular-sized strips, each embroidered with flowers and birds and lined with gold wires on both sides. There was another kind of skirt called the hundred-pleat skirt, which was made of one piece of cloth folded into wrinkles." The designs of these skirts have been passed down as a fashion item through the Qing Dynasty to the Republic of China (1912–49) and right down to the present day.

Effects of Delicate Costume

The *qipao* was a fashion mainstay in the Qing Dynasty. The many different *qipao* worn by actress Maggie Cheung in the film *In the Mood for Love* are representative of this iconic Chinese garment for many people, however the *qipao* in the Han ethnic style, which became popular after 1912, is not the same as those worn by Manchu women when the Qing Dynasty was established. To distinguish the two kinds of *qipao,* we will refer to the latter as Manchu nationality women's dress.

With the establishment of the Qing Dynasty capital in Beijing, the Manchu and Han nationality costume cultures began to integrate. According to historical records, "In 1652, the imperial order *Clothing Colour and Palanquin Regulations* was issued, and clothes of Han nationality style disappeared. In the Ming Dynasty, men wore their hair long and in the form of a top-knot, loose clothes, stockings and shallow-faced shoes; in the Qing Dynasty, men who did not belong to the Manchu nationality were required to shave the top of their head leaving a long pigtail at the back, and wear long tight-fitting robes with narrow sleeves, tight socks and long boots."

The Manchu people led a nomadic life before crossing the Shanhai Pass from Northeast China to settle in the heartland of China. The Manchu traditional dress facilitating riding and shooting were different from the Han nationality's loose-fitting dress. The Qing rulers believed the convenience and simplicity of Manchu dress determined that they could fight and win repeatedly. So, they focused on preserving, protecting and developing their ethnic costumes.

Manchu dress has been described in this way, "The Manchu costumes are rectangular. The saddle-shaped collar protects cheek and face. The costume doesn't show the waistline, with the shirt not shown outside. Round buttons decorate the right front of a garment. There are two to three sleeves for decoration. Fringes decorate the sleeve ends.... the modelling is complete and well-knit in the shape of a closed box. Therefore, the figure under the Qing costume looks decent and unique, changing the tower-shaped clothing worn for thousands of years and leaving a deep impression on us."

The Qing Dynasty was also the dynasty that interacted most with other countries. The collision and integration of western and oriental cultures stimulated that interaction. Qing dress absorbed the essence of the ethnic Han culture inherited by the Ming Dynasty. In addition, Manchu dress rules established a new type of Chinese style. Detailed and complex rules and regulations governed everything from the formal attire of Qing emperors and officials to the conventional folk attire. In the contemporary era, you can still see the influence of Qing dress in imperial robes, embroidered robes, *qipao* and various fineries.

There are countless examples in terms of Qing dress style, material, tailoring and dressmaking techniques and wearing regulations. The official dress in the Qing Dynasty continued to use the mandarin square. Women's clothing underwent the greatest change from the Ming Dynasty. They were mainly in the Manchu style, long shirt, long robe, flared pants and wide-plait skirt. This kind of costume usually had a crossover collar, with the front of a garment finishing on the right-hand side. Wide fringes were used to decorate the collar, front of the garment and sleeves. The sleeves were short with a wide end at the cuffs. The robe was slit down the sides, and worn with wide-ended big pants and flowerpot-shaped shoes. The long robes and long skirts loved by women in the Ming Dynasty remained the mainstream in terms of costume.

Besides the Manchu costumes, women in the Qing Dynasty wore long robes and long shirts with pleated skirts, which reached to the feet. Beneath the skirt, they wore wide-ended big pants. It is worth noting women in the Qing Dynasty wore a kind of cloak named the *"yikouzhong,"* which had no sleeves or cleavage and several types of collar designs. The cloak was decorated with bright-coloured silks and satins and diverse patterns. Some types of collars were decorated with a fur fringe, the lining of which was warm and soft designer fur.

In winter, the cloak covered the whole body, except the neck and head, which could both keep out the cold and show the beauty of the female form. Another costume was the *"yunjian,"* a decoration worn on women's shoulders. Initially, girls in the Qing Dynasty applied *yunjian* to their wedding outfits. Later on, girls in Southeast China used *yunjian* as a shield against their dangling hair knots to keep their clothes neat. It developed into a decoration for noblewomen, who combined it with silk threads, pearls and other precious stones.

The techniques for making Qing dress reached a very high level. In the Palace Museum in Beijing is a work of art titled "Horse-Riding Portrait," by the Italian artist Giuseppe Castiglione, showing Emperor Qianlong reviewing troops at Nanyuan. The drawing depicts the emperor's impressive armour. Qing armour consisted of the outer coat of armour, the clothing worn inside the armour and a helmet. The *"dayuejia,"* meaning parade armour, is the most exquisite form of armour. *Dayuejia* is not made of metal. Instead, golden threads were used to embroider golden patterns on the yellow satin to replace the golden leaves on the armour. The helmet was "made of cow leather, decorated by painting, embedded with pearls, and decorated with golden sanskrit. The clothing inside the armour is decorated with a pattern of dragons playing with pearls, with a golden pattern in the interval and dragons on the fringe. The round-shaped heart protector is surrounded by a dragon and cloud pattern."

Among the costume relics left by China's long list of dynasties, the Qing Dynasty is the best represented, and this has had a profound impact on the modern and contemporary dress culture and the folk costume styles in Beijing.

From 1153, when Jin emperor Hailingwang (reign: 1150–61) made Beijing his capital, to the termination of the last feudal dynasty in China, the Qing Dynasty witnessed both the cultural changes of the city and the evolution of Chinese dress. Fashion is a cornerstone of history. By touching each detail, you may see the never-ending pursuit of a happy life by generations of Chinese people.

Postscript

With Beijing reaching its 860th anniversary as a capital, it is difficult to condense so much history into a single magazine, but it is an honour and a source of pride to record Beijing's splendid and glorious culture and extensive and profound history, and it is a marvelous opportunity to review Beijing's past.

Credit and thanks are due to those who created abundant ancient civilization; to the scholars who recorded the city's extensive and profound history; to those who devote themselves to the goal of turning Beijing into World City with Chinese characteristics. Because of them, Beijing remains brilliant and can look forward to a brighter future.

References

Living Memory of Beijing City, Hou Renzhi, China Publishing Group Corporation, Joint Bookstore, September 2009

History of Liao Dynasty (All Five Volumes), Zhonghua Book Company, the punctuated edition, May 2011

History of Jin Dynasty (All Eight Volumes), Zhonghua Book Company, the punctuated edition, March 2011

History of Yuan Dynasty (All 15 Volumes), Zhonghua Book Company, 1976

Meng Sen's Lectures on Ming Dynasty, Meng Sen, Zhonghua Book Company, May 2009

History of Ming Dynasty (All Eight Volumes), Wan Sitong, Shanghai Guji Press, January 2008.

Three Hundred Years of Ming Dynasty, Wu Han, International Culture Publishing Company, October 2011

The Cambridge History of China Vol. 8: The Ming Dynasty, 1368-1644, (Complete Version), Frederick W. Mote, Denis Twitchett, translated by Zhang Shusheng, China Social Sciences Press, February 1992

Travels of Marco Polo, translated by Feng Chengjun, The Commercial Press, June 2012

The First Half of My Life, Aixinjueluo, Puyi, Qunzhong Press, January 2013

Twilight in the Forbidden City; Reginald Fleming Johnston, translated by Qin Chuan'an; Central Compilation and Translation Press; April 2010

Essays on Liao and Jin Dynasties (Part IX); edited by Xu Zhenqing, Jia Yunjiang; Zhongzhou Guji Press, 1996

Essays on the Study of Jin Dynasty, (an thesis collection of the second Jin Dynasty International Academic Symposium), edited by Pai Haichun, Wang Yulang, Ha'rbin Press, 2000

Articles in Liao and Jin Dynasties (All Three Volumes), Yan Fengwu, Shanxi Guji Press, 1999

The Poetry in Liao and Jin Dynasties (All Three Volumes); Yan Fengwu, Kang Jinsheng; Shanxi Guji Press; 2002

Archives for Song, Liao, and Jin Dynasties (Volume I); Research Office of Song, Liao, Jin, and Yuan Dynasties, Institute of History, China Social Sciences; Zhonghua Book Company; 1985

Archives for Song, Liao, and Jin Dynasties (Volume II); Research Office of Song, Liao, Jin, and Yuan Dynasties, Institute of History, China Social Sciences; Zhonghua Book Company, 1991

The Comments on Wanyan Liang, Zhou Feng, The Ethnic Publishing House, 2002

The Biography of Jin Shizong, Liu Suyong, Sanqin Press. 1986

The Biography of Jin Zhangzong; Fan Jun, Zhou Feng; China Radio and Television Publishing House, 2003

Essays on Literature of Jin Dynasty, Zhou Huiquan, Northeast Normal University Press, 1997

Study on Literature of Liao, Jin and Yuan Dynasties; Li Zhengmin, Dong Guoyan; Culture and Art Publishing House, 1999

Capital of Jin Dynast; Yu Jie, Yu Guang; Beijing Publishing House, 1989

The Biography of Yuan Haowen; Hao Shuhou, Yang Guoyong; Shanxi People's Publishing House, 1990

The Proofed Version of Jin Dynasty (Complete Edition), author: Yuwen Maozhao, proofed by Cui Wenyin, Zhonghua Book Company, 1986

The History of Khitan State, author: Ye Longlu; punctuated by Jia Jingyan, Lin Ronggui, Shanghai Guji Publishing House, 1985

The History of Chinese Drama, Xu Muyun, Shanghai Guji Publishing House, February 2001

Chinese Operas in Song and Yuan Dynasties, Wang Guowei, Zhonghua Book Company, August 2010

A history of Chinese Drama, translated by Bu He, Peking University Press, July 2011

Yiguantianxia: History of Chinese Costume with Pictures; Huang Nengfu, Qiao Qiaoling; Zhonghua Book Company; November 2009

Study on Chinese Ancient Costumes, Shen Congwen, Shanghai Bookstore Press, January 2011

The Notes on Qing Dynasty, Meng Sen, Zhonghua Book Company, January 2010

History of Qing Dynasty, Zheng Tianting, Tianjin People's Publishing House May 2011

The Sixteen Lectures on Qing Dynasty, Wang Zhonghan, Zhonghua Book Company, January 2009

The Biography of Qing Dynasty, Zhonghua Book Company. the 11th edition, 1987

A General Survey of Chinese Poetry, Zhao Minli, People's Literature Publishing House, The fifth edition, May 2013

The Notes on the History of Chinese Painting and Calligraphy; Zhu Heping, Guo Mengliang; Zhongzhou Guji Press, December 2009

Chinese Calligraphy History: Volume of Song, Liao and Jin Dynasties, Cao Baolin, Jiangsu Education Press, April 2009

Chinese Calligraphy History: Volume of Yuan and Ming Dynasties, Huang Chun, Jiangsu Education Press, April 2009

Chinese Calligraphy History: Volume of Qing Dynasty, Liu Heng, Jiangsu Education Press, April 2009

The relevant thesis from Peking University, Renmin University of China, Fudan University and others are referred to as well.

北京城纪

BEIJING'S HISTORICAL STORIES

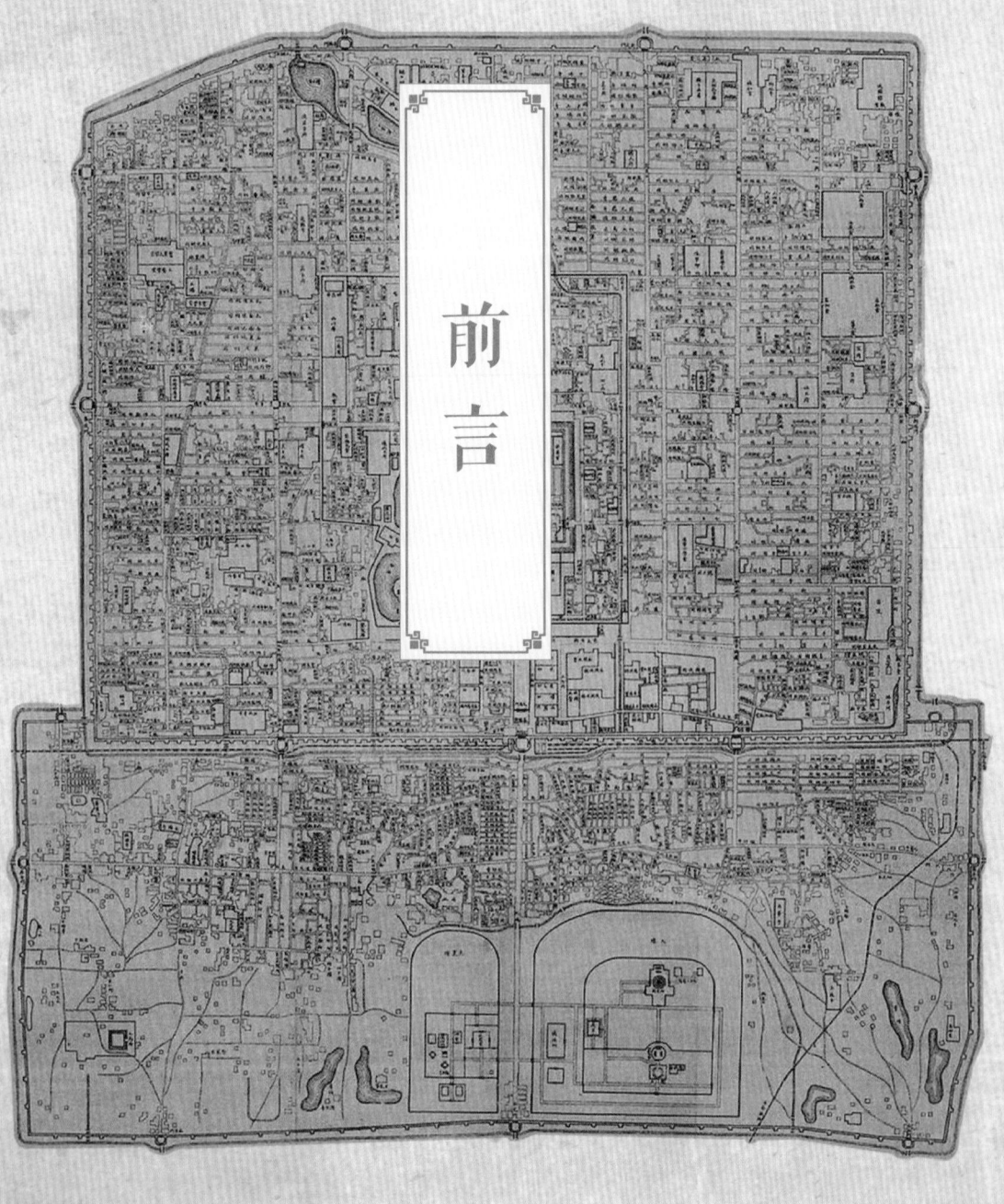

前言

今天，北京是中华人民共和国的首都；860多年前，中国金朝（1115—1234年）皇帝海陵王完颜亮（1122—1161年）率领着他的子民跨越白山黑水迁都这里，命名为金中都，开启了这座城市的都城史。

今天，北京是中国的首善之区，在打造中国特色世界城市的道路上锐意进取；860多年前，开启都城史的北京已拥有完整而科学的都城形制，皇家文化从此发端。

今天，北京是世界瞩目的设计之都，古老的建筑遗产与见证着现代化发展的新地标和谐共存；860多年前，金中都为北京奠定了皇城风范，一路行至元朝（1271—1368年），壮美的中轴线和前朝后市、左祖右社的壮阔城市引世人折腰，成就黄金之国的绝美传奇并为后世所续写。

今天，北京是包容世界文明的文化之都，与世界共享并共同创造异彩纷呈的文化精粹；860多年前，"为天地立心，为生民立命，为往圣继绝学，为万世开太平"的理念已经在这里生根发芽，并经由一代代文化精英传承、发展，由此缔造了北京独特而灿烂的都城文明。

今天，北京是海纳百川且时时刻刻为世界人民带来惊喜的时尚之都；860多年前，华夏子民的爱美之心已体现在衣食住行的各个方面，为北京奉献了无数霓裳嘉韵、艺苑群英。

……

860余年都城史，滋养着北京这片厚土的人杰地灵，书写着北京历史的波澜壮阔，收藏着北京文化的博大精深，见证着北京穿越历史风烟、在对传统的继承和对未来的创造中披荆斩棘，奋勇前行。

860余年都城史，是北京的辉煌，是北京人的骄傲。860余年都城史犹如一本厚重的大书，她的边边角角无一不值得珍藏和记取，而写在时光边上的光辉岁月，让这本令人敬畏又令人激动的大书于一开一合之际，无上荣光。

这里是北京。

章节·伍 丹青 炫墨而舞

画千般美景 终不过面向汉文化一番膜拜　72
画四时佳期 不外穷毕生功力开一代先河　74
画京畿胜景 袭古人启变法成繁荣之风　76
画万方智慧 树一国经典蕴后世中兴　80
　84

章节·陆 绮韵 寄世而吟

生逢艰难时世总是诗人的福气　88
文理与世推移江山代有诗词歌赋　90
盛世乱世身为重臣者常有写意情怀　94
人生如初见便山山水水成十万诗篇　98
　102

章节·柒 霓裳 嘉韵天成

镶珠绣金山林熊虎皆入画成衫　106
不缕金堆绣无侍儿搀扶怎说奢华　108
布衣皇帝制服饰等级难掩别有洞天　110
一口钟罩不住精致华美艳惊后世　114
　118

后记

122

目录

章节·壹 魔方 众城之城

- 首次定都 跨越白山黑水的远征 — 06
- 盛世大都 隐形黄金之国的惊世繁华 — 08
- 紫禁雄风 天工不必巧夺暂借无妨 — 10
- 14

章节·贰 厚土 藏龙之地

- 欲经营天下驻跸之所非燕不可 — 18
- 圣上龙兴之地 帝王万世之都 — 22
- 龙穴砂水形势理气诸吉咸备 — 26
- 32

章节·叁 至尊 豪杰之所

- 燕都的热土或许适宜栽种莲花 — 36
- 黄金之城住不下征伐不息的灵魂 — 38
- 热血英雄被供奉得久了也便成为神 — 42
- 伤城之内满园深浅色总是旧河山 — 46
- 50

章节·肆 笙歌 踏戏而行

- 太平多暇 干戈倒载闲兵甲 — 54
- 瓦舍勾栏 怒说千古兴亡事 — 56
- 民间传奇 花花草草由人恋 — 60
- 徽汉合流 京腔京韵自多情 — 64
- 68

章节·壹

魔方 众城之城

随着摄影机的位置缓缓上升，紧盯监视器的他渐渐坐直了身子。这是个神奇的时刻，一座城池正在显示它逐渐"下沉"时的魅力。数次乘飞机抵达这个东方都会，他从未如此直接地将它尽收眼底。"这是一座魔方般的城市"，他这样表达对北京的感悟——它恢弘大气的形制规范令人屏息凝神。

多年以后的2011年，他坐着轮椅出现在法国戛纳电影节上，获得终身成就奖。他说，他因"爱上"中国文化而受益。他是意大利人，名叫贝尔纳多·贝特鲁奇。1986年8月16日，他在北京开始拍摄一部"最费工夫"的电影，即此后斩获无数大奖的《末代皇帝》，他本人也因这个中国故事而成为第一位获准进入故宫拍摄电影的外国导演。

此后，他向在改革开放之初尚没有机会亲睹北京的外国人持续地传递一个简单却充满诱惑的信息——北京是魔方。

这是个恰当的比喻。北京的确是从一座方方正正的"城邦"发展而来。860余年建都史上每一次建设、扩张、繁荣、改造直至将这座城市"加工"成型，都仿佛魔方上一个个小小"插件"转动与啮合得严丝合缝，日臻完美。

首次定都 跨越白山黑水的远征

金

一一五五至一二三四

章节·壹 魔方 众城之城

关于北京建都史的起点研究，至今有两次最令人兴奋的考古发现。

第一次是1990年10月。北京市园林局在右安门外玉林小区盖宿舍时，偶然发现金中都南城墙水关遗址。这是当年的全国十大考古发现之一。北京市人民政府当即决定在这里建设辽金城垣博物馆。水关是古代城墙下供河水进出的水道建筑。金中都水关遗址是一处正南北方向的木、石结构建筑，上半部已被毁掉，只残存基础。至今，这是已发现的中国古代都城水关遗址中规模最大的一处，是研究古代建筑和水利设施的重要实例，同时也进一步确定了金中都南城墙的确切位置。

第二次是2010年6月3日。对于北京来说这是具有特殊意义的一天，正在建设中的丽泽金融商务区发掘出面积近1000平方米的金中都遗址，这一地块位于丰台区凤凰嘴村的北部，南距凤凰嘴村金中都城墙遗址公园21米。大量的考古发掘成果将北京的建都史研究带入新阶段。

这两次大规模考古发掘之间相隔20年，然而北京人对于金中都遗址、遗迹以及隐匿于北京各处的文化遗存的寻觅和探究从未停止过。

2003年，为纪念北京建都850周年，在原金中都大安殿旧址上建成北京建都纪念阙，确认了北京正式成为都城的历史开启于1153年4月21日，也就是中国金代第四位皇帝海陵王完颜亮一声令下让他的子民跨越白山黑水定居于这片土地的那一天。

时光退回到860多年前，以弑君夺得皇位的完颜亮已无需靠题诗书写对于"黄袍加身"的渴求，而只需仔细设计作为国君当如何安基立业。于是，他做出了对他自己和对后来叫作"北京"的这座城市都极为重要的一个决定——迁都。深受汉文化影响又热衷于民族融合的他，因此成为北京建都史上的开天辟地者。虽然史书中的完颜亮野心勃勃、嗜杀成性，但对于帝都，他的贡献是无可争议的，他从一开始就确立了将北京建造成一座包容且时尚、充满设计韵味的开放型都城。作为皇帝，完颜亮的一生也是精心到苛刻地打造都城的一生。《金史》中记载，为了建造都城花费大量人力、财力，"运一木之费至二千万，率一车之力至五百人"。而皇城之豪华今人只能凭借文字展开想象，"宫殿之饰，遍傅黄金而后间以五彩，金屑飞空如落雪。一殿之费以亿万计，成而复毁，务极华丽"。

作为金代都城，北京只有61年的辉煌。此后历经几个朝代，无论歌舞升平还是战火纷飞，走过的路太长，一路丢失的东西难免很多。

2001年，北京辽金城垣博物馆对北京地区辽金遗迹展开调查。走遍整座北京城，认定北京现存辽代的地上建筑仅有15座辽塔，金代的地上建筑除9座金塔外，还有一座卢沟桥。辽金时期的墓幢共有19项，经幢共发现了30余项，遗址遗迹类共计30余处，还发现了18座辽金时期的石碑、5函舍利石函、墓志11块。

与北京灿烂的皇城文化相比，这些遗存的确显得少了些，但是，完颜亮和他的王朝以另一种方式"长驻"北京。他们留下了大量名胜古迹，显示着他们在征战之余的闲情雅致。今天尚存的北海、香山、钓鱼台、玉泉山、陶然亭、玉渊潭等，都是当年金朝皇帝的离宫别苑。今天人们所津津乐道的"燕京八景"之太液秋风、琼岛春荫、西山晴雪、卢沟晓月、玉泉垂虹等，也是从金朝开始出现的。

元 盛世大都 隐形黄金之国的惊世繁华

一二七一至一三六八

章节·壹 魔方 众城之城

"元大都全城的设计都用直线规划。大体上，所有街道全是笔直走向，直达城根。一个人若登城站在城门上，朝正前方远望，便可看见对面城墙的城门。城内公共街道两侧，有各种各样的商店和货摊……整个城市按四方形布置，如同一块棋盘。"《马可·波罗游记》中对元大都的记载颇多，如果马可·波罗能穿越时光在今日向世界说明北京，恐怕他也会用上"魔方"二字——他笔下的城池，是魔方的早期形制。

在各种史料图画的记载中，元大都是一座"世界城邦"，其开放程度达到了同一历史时期全世界之罕见。来自天南海北，说着不同方言的商人、武士、职业旅行家、外交使节、传教士、手艺人等各色人等云集于此，自由生活，自由贸

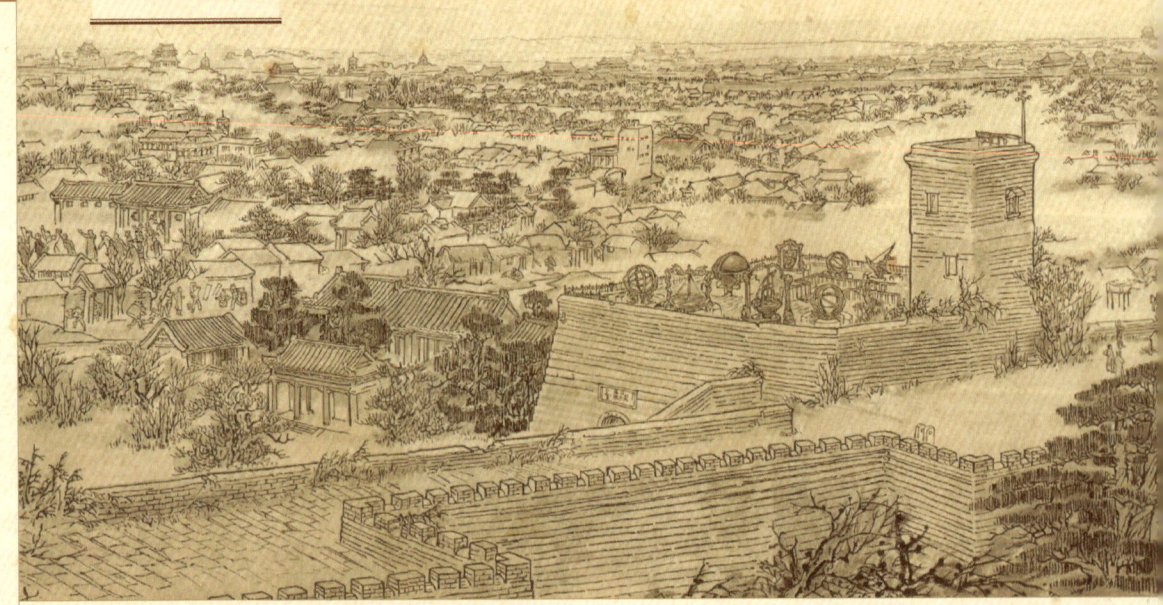

易，和谐相处，自得其乐。对此，《马可·波罗游记》中也有描述："每个城郊在距城墙约一英里的地方都建有旅馆或招待骆驼商队的大旅店，可提供各地往来商人的居住之所，并且不同的人都住在不同的指定的住所，而这些住所又是相互隔开的。例如一种住所指定给伦巴人，另一种指定给德意志人，第三种指定给法兰西人……每当有外国专使来到大都，如果他们负有与大汗利益相关的任务，则他们照例是由皇家招待的。"

中国元代的历史向来以民族融合和文明交汇吸引着全世界史家的目光，而众多中外史学家一致认为，元大都作为一声呼哨啸聚天下铁骑的元代皇帝坐镇江山之处，不仅是一国之都，更是众城之城。成吉思汗（1162—1227年）和他的后裔征服了东自中国、西抵多瑙河畔的大片土地，不仅扩大版图，扫清沿途各国边境线的障碍，更疏导了东西方的交通。世界范围内的几大古老文明像河流一样在这里交汇、碰撞，而这座城市也像它的主人一样显示

了博大胸襟，将一切文明元素笑纳于怀中，兼收并蓄，化为己用。

写出了著名的早期畅销书《马可·波罗游记》的马可·波罗（1254—1324年）一定对元大都有着深厚的感情，他在书中描写过皇城、皇宫、广场、街道、城墙、城门，等等，不一而足。幸亏有他的这些记载，才能让后人看到一个华丽王朝究竟是怎样一番景象。在他的笔下，元大都"整体呈正方形，周长二十四英里，每边为六英里，有一土城墙围绕全城。城墙底宽十步，愈向上则愈窄，到墙顶，宽不过三步。城垛全是白色的。城中的全部设计都以直线为主，所以各条街道都沿一条直线，直达城墙根。一个人若登上城门，向街上望去，就可以看见对面城墙的城门。在城里的大道两旁有各色各样的商店和铺子。全城建屋所占的土地也都是四方形的，并且彼此在一条直线上，每块地都有充分的空间来建造美丽的住宅、庭院和花园"。这是何等美轮美奂的乌托邦！

遗憾的是，马可·波罗和众多国外旅行家们笔下的那个呈现了惊世繁荣的黄金之国、帝王之城已经成为静待后人研究、发掘的"隐形城市"。对于今日的北京人来说，从1957年开始发掘、保护、修建、复建至2006年暂告一段落并形成"大都盛景"的北京元大都城垣遗址公园，才是目前唯一能窥见中国历史上这个巨型帝国之风光的遗迹。公元1271年，忽必烈（1215—1294年）取《易经》"大哉乾元"之意，建国号元，同时下诏定都燕京，称大都。元朝的版图一度北达北冰洋，东临日本海，西逾葱岭，南接交趾（今越南），造就了世界历史上空前绝后的泱泱大国。而今，元城新象、大都鼎盛、龙泽鱼跃、双都巡幸、四海宾朋、海棠花溪、安定生辉、水街华灯、角楼古韵等景区组成了在元大都土城遗址上建造起来的城市带状公园,供人们循着史书和传说的路径,凭吊一代天骄成吉思汗。

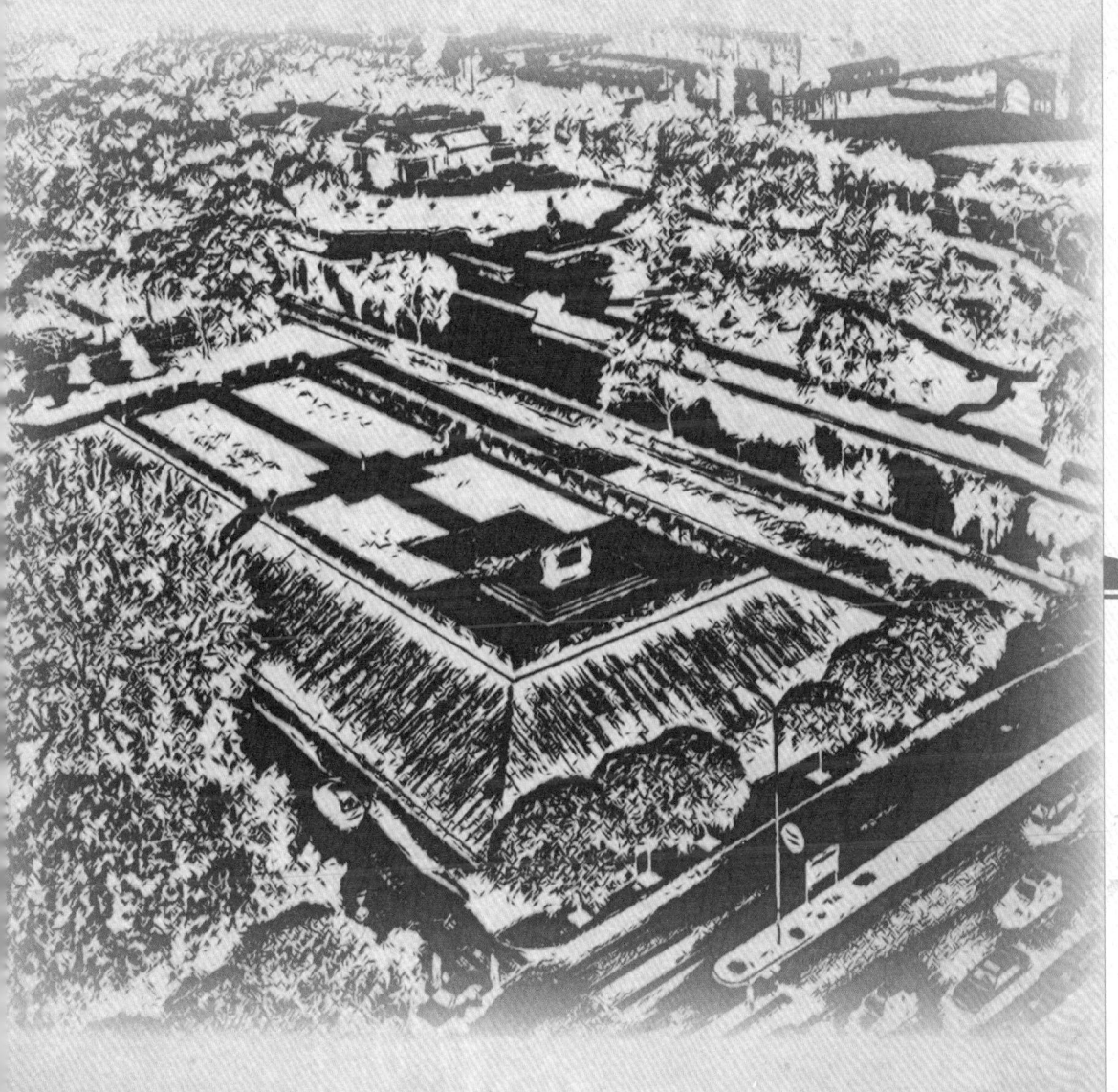

章节·壹　魔方　众城之城

明清 紫禁雄风 天工不必巧夺暂借无妨

一三六八至一九一一

"世界上像北京设计得这么方方正正、匀匀称称的城市，还没见过。因为住惯了这样布局齐整得几乎像棋盘似的地方，一去外省，老是迷路转向。瞧，这儿以紫禁城（故宫）为中心，九门对称，前有天安，后有地安，东西便门就相当于足球场上踢角球的位置。北城有钟鼓二楼，四面是天地日月坛。街道则东单西单、南北池子……"早年负笈英伦且做过第二次世界大战战地记者的中国作家萧乾在其《北京城杂忆》一文中对北京城市"规制"如此描写。他笔下这个"方方正正"的城市，便是明清以降因遗迹处处可见而为今人所熟悉的北京——一个日渐成型、相对稳定的魔方。

元代最后一位皇帝抵挡不住明朝大将徐达的威猛，弃城而去，再度成为蒙古草原上一名顺水草而居的牧者。攻克了元大都的徐达则受命兴建燕王府以迎接明朝开国皇帝朱元璋的四儿子燕王朱棣北上兴国。明永乐元年（1403年）正月，礼部尚书李至刚上奏："自昔帝王，或起布衣定天下，或由外藩入承大统，其于肇迹之地皆有升崇。窃见北平布政司实皇上承运兴王之地，宜遵太祖高皇帝中都之制，立为京都。"据史书记载，李至刚一度在迁都的问题上旁征博引以说服永乐皇帝，他列举了历史上很多关于选定国都的"经验"，比如《吕氏春秋·审分览·知度》载："古

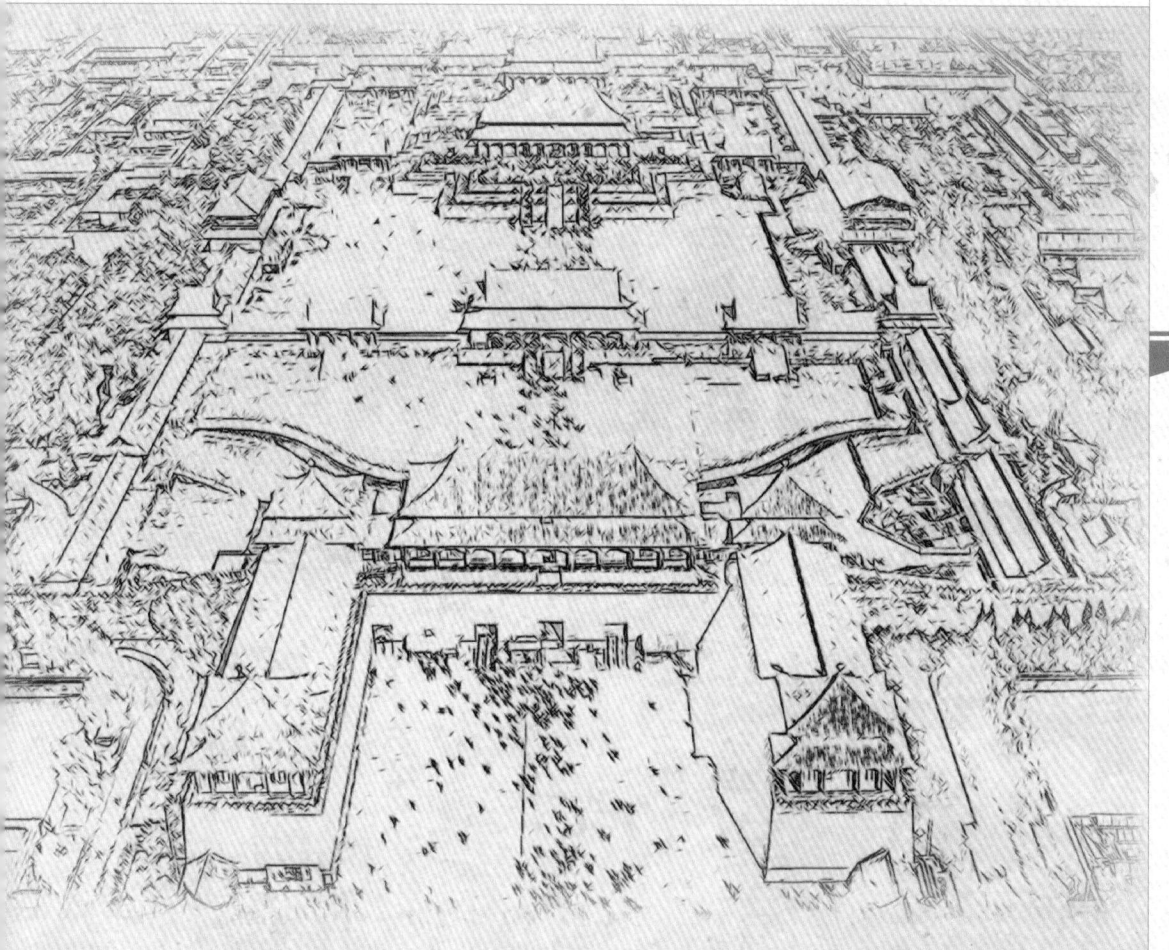

之王者，择天下之中而立国，择国之中而立宫"，《管子·乘马》又载："凡立国都，非于大山之下，必于广川之上。高毋近旱，而水用足；下毋近水，而沟防省。"山环水抱、气场强大的北京"东临辽碣，西依太行，北连朔漠，背扼军都，南控中原"，恰是天下难觅的风水宝地。历史总是充满巧合与玄机，尽管今天，元大都的沧虹已远，但对于当年的永乐皇帝来说，其繁华仍是黄粱梦中美景，更何况若想平定中原，必不能不占据军机要地以镇北方。于是，明永乐十九年（1421年），曾经的元大都正式定名为北京，成为明朝首都，并自此从未改变其一国之都的显赫地位。

北京明清以来的建筑奇观数不胜数，而在北京作为明清帝都的建筑史上，有两个名号响亮非常——蒯祥和"样式雷"。细细盘点北京那些成为城市经典的古代建筑，他们和他们率领的团队，参与设计和建设的数量占一半以上。

在大多数史料记载中，明代最著名的建筑设计师蒯祥是天安门的设计者。明永乐十五年（1417年），蒯祥先期北上参加皇宫建筑设计并且被任命为皇宫重大工程的设计师。他的第一项任务是设计和组织施工作为宫廷正门的承天门（即今之天安门）。蒯祥在皇帝正式定都的大日子之前出色完成任务，永乐皇帝龙颜大悦，称他为"蒯鲁班"。从此，他开始了作为皇家首席建筑设计师的灿烂职业生涯。蒯祥在京40多年，曾负责兴建紫禁城内的前三殿（即现在的太和、中和、保和三大殿）。很不幸，这三大殿于1457年被大火烧毁。八年后，明英宗请他重建九开二层的木构城楼，以及两宫、五府、六衙署等。1464年他主持明十三陵中的裕陵建造。蒯祥有功于朝廷，从一名工匠逐步晋升，直至被封为工部左侍郎，授二品官，享一品官俸禄。据明史及有关建筑专著评介，身居高位的蒯祥在建筑学上的造诣炉火纯青。他将江南建筑艺术巧妙运用，苏州彩画、琉璃金砖在建筑中的运用都自蒯祥始。可以说，他亲手造就了金碧辉煌的北京城。

2012年初，54岁的"样式雷"第十代孙、体育教师雷章宝在接受《北京》杂志记者采访时，含蓄地表达了对雷氏先人的敬仰和对传承、保护和宣传"样式雷"遗产的希望。事实上，对于大多数熟识北京清代皇家苑囿却并不熟识北京建筑史的人来说，"样式雷"是一个陌生的概念。

建筑大师梁思成在《中国建筑与中国建筑师》一书中曾写道:"在清朝北京皇室的建筑师成了世袭的职位……这个世袭的建筑师家族被称为'样式雷'。"2007年9月,"样式雷"成为中国入选的第五个"世界记忆遗产"项目,终于隆重地走进人们的视线。至今,在故宫的高墙之内,仍保存着'样式雷'图档。简单材料所制成的烫样,其原理与现代建筑的三维空间设计如出一辙。从清康熙皇帝开始直至清末两百年间,雷氏共八代人主持了皇家建筑设计,宫殿、苑囿、陵寝以及衙署、庙宇无不在内,包括被列入世界遗产名录的故宫、天坛、颐和园、承德避暑山庄、清东陵和西陵,以及圆明园等的建筑设计,也都出自雷氏家族。故宫收藏的83件烫样形象逼真、数据准确,主要是清代同治、光绪年间重建圆明园、颐和园、西苑等地时所做的设计模型。据目前的考古发现显示,"样式雷"图档很可能是中国古代建筑史上仅有的档案记载。深谙风水学和建筑文化的"样式雷"家族将北京的皇家建筑"规范"成一派外呈恢弘大气、内现精雕细琢、融端庄秀丽为一体的皇朝风格,又因选址的讲究和精到将北京的山水城郭运用得恰到好处。可以说,雷氏家族亲手造就了天人合一的北京。

城市的建筑是凝固的历史。自1949年成为中华人民共和国的首都至今,北京城这只魔方经历了并正在经历着飞旋般的变化。新的城市地标不断涌现,古老与现代和谐并存,而在这座城市中岿然不动的是那些历经岁月的古代遗迹,它们是曾经辉煌的城市文明史的注脚,也是正在辉煌的北京步入世界一流城市行列的见证。

章节·贰
厚土 藏龙之地

加里·吉盖克斯（Gary Gygax）曾是一名保险推销员。偶尔，推销员无需面对他致力于发展的客户并以三寸不烂之舌说服对方直至将他的钱变成一张能让自己挣钱的保险单，这样的时刻，他疲惫而孤独。他懒得说话，他自己和自己玩儿。世界上有无数保险推销员在此时选择了沉默、发呆、饮酒催眠……加里·吉盖克斯却有幸成为一朵奇葩，他发明了最早的桌上角色扮演游戏（TRPG）——《龙与地下城》。

1974年《龙与地下城》游戏诞生，2008年3月4日加里·吉盖克斯在家中去世，数以亿计的玩家和后继开发者始终感激并怀念他。同时，在遥远的东方——中国，有一群不仅玩过游戏，而且还看过以游戏名字命名的电影且对其中的神龙、恶龙念念不忘的人，在观念上与他不谋而合。龙，从来与看不见的城池紧密相连，无论飞龙在天还是潜龙入地，所谓见首不见尾，那是另一个世界。

失去了加里·吉盖克斯的世界一度有过短暂的热闹，人们猜测，他的龙和地下城究竟是源于西方文化还是源于爱看闲书的他偶然邂逅的中国龙的某个故事？争执之际，一个埋伏在中国历史中已超过700年的名字被数度提起——刘伯温，这位明朝开国时一人之下、万人之上的高官，也是众口一词公认最聪明的人。在传说中，玉帝派他前往人间铲除妖孽，助大明朝一统天下。于是，在人们的口耳相传中，他降服了苦海幽州的孽龙，建造了"内九外七皇城四，前门楼子在正中"的北京城；他是北京建都史上最早的"降魔人"，赶走恶龙的他此后又为皇帝精心挑选了陵寝所在，让明朝的十三位"真龙天子"安息于如今已列入世界遗产名录的北京明十三陵。无论这一切是否是正史，至少有一点可谓真切，那就是此后，明十三陵的辉煌豪华引发了清代皇帝的效仿，从而缔造了曾经在北京版图之上现在河北省境内的巨大皇家陵园清东陵和清西陵，将清代的帝后妃嫔"一网打尽"。

传说与史实究竟相去多远，很难考证，然而，伫立于北京的一处处皇家陵寝一直在昭告世人，北京以真实的历史，演绎着名副其实的"龙与地下城"。

章节·贰 厚土 藏龙之地

金元 欲经营天下驻跸之所非燕不可

一一五至一三六八

860余年前，也就是公元1153年，金国海陵王完颜亮不远千里迁都北京，定名为金中都，开启了北京作为国都的历史。

据史料记载，完颜亮虽然弑君夺位、能征惯战且杀人不眨眼，但同时他还是一位善于学习、热衷阅读、博闻强记的人，他喜欢汉文化，认为汉文化中有女真人一统江山的前程。这样说来，他选择北京定都，应该是经过了深入细致的研究和深思熟虑。

史料中有关于完颜亮请"高人"解析北京风水的传说。而这些为皇帝出谋划策的人，举出的例子大多来自汉文化典籍。例如，唐代地理学家杨益如此定义北京的山川风物："燕山最高，象天市，盖北干之正结。其龙发昆仑之中脉，绵亘数千里……以地理之法论之，其龙势之长，垣局之美，干龙大尽，山水大会……最合法度。"地理学家只说山形水势，不论堪舆之学，如果能有理学家辅助一说，则说服力大增。这样，到了宋代，大学者朱熹有了进一步解释："冀都是天地间好个大风水。山脉从云中发来，前面黄河环绕，泰山耸左为龙，华山耸右为虎，嵩山为前案，淮南诸山为第二重案，江南五岭为第三重案，故古今建都之地，皆莫过于冀都。"如此，此时不占领这风水宝地，更待何时？

2002年，北京市文物局发布消息称在北

京房山区大房山麓发掘出的金陵，是中国历史上为数不多的少数民族皇陵，也是北京地区年代最早、规模最大的帝王陵。经过金海陵王完颜亮、世宗、章宗、卫绍王、宣宗五世超过60年的营建，形成面积约60平方公里的大型皇家陵寝。在此之后，在金陵主陵区即房山区周口店镇龙门口村北的九龙山，发掘出金太祖完颜阿骨打的陵墓。其时陵墓打开，发现"完颜阿骨打的龙椁已残毁，仅保留椁盖和东壁挡板，上面刻着团龙纹及流云纹。凤椁位于龙椁北侧，为整块汉白玉雕凿而成。盖顶及椁身刻有双凤纹，内填金粉，椁身四壁裹松香。石椁内放置着一具木棺，外壁涂红漆，四角及正中部位有菱形鎏金银饰，上錾刻凤鸟纹。在南北两侧的银饰件上对称铆有两个铁环"。考古人员还发现，发掘出的棺内残留有头骨及下肢骨，随葬有一件金丝凤冠，纹饰极为精美。在金太祖陵西南，同时还发现了5座陪葬墓。

金陵的发现让后人明了了一件事，原来完颜亮入主金中都后，在发展经济、建设都城之余，他一直在忙碌着为几位逝去先皇选择完美阴宅，同时也为自己百年之后的安居未雨绸缪。在有关金陵的考古发掘报告中介绍，完颜亮在北京建立金中都后，决定将原在黑龙江阿城的祖陵迁至北京。他曾专门派出司天台的官员在北京寻找风水宝地，后来终于选定房山区的金陵现址。按照堪舆学的解释，这里背靠的大山是玄武，左边和右边的山包分别是青龙和白虎，前面的案山间被人工挖成一道暗渠，也就是所谓的朱雀。无疑，这令海陵王龙颜大悦，因此他对这处陵寝十分重视，在建设期间曾前来视察4次，最后一次更驻扎半个月亲自监工。1155年十月，金陵竣工，完颜亮将包括金太祖完颜阿骨打在内的先皇"迁居"到此。

女真人历来勇猛善战，金太祖定国号为"金"，基于屡屡将其打败的"辽"字面意思为"铁"。完颜阿骨打一生驰骋疆场，他的梦想便是灭契丹辽国，直捣中原灭掉北宋，以金克铁，无往而不胜。然而，最终，金太祖功败垂成，没能等到梦想成真。好在他的子孙中有完颜亮这样的传奇人物。随着他的棺椁落户北京，他终于可以在另一个世界里笑望中原。

中国的帝王历来自有其生死观，生前呼风唤雨，死后抵达彼岸仍要保持生前的威仪和排场，因此，中国的帝王陵寝规模、形制很多时候若不是超越了执掌江山时的规格，至少也要保持与之一致。

北京的都城史自金代始，此后经历了元、明、清，以辛亥革命结束帝制实现共和终。四个皇朝中，唯有元代，在目

孛儿只斤·忽必烈（1215－1294年），蒙古族，元朝的创建者，是监国托雷第四子，元宪宗蒙哥弟，蒙古尊号"薛禅汗"。青年时代，他便"思大有为于天下"。孛儿只斤·忽必烈建立了幅员辽阔的统一多民族国家元朝。他在位期间，建立行省制，加强中央集权，使得社会经济逐渐恢复和发展。他也曾多次派兵侵略邻国，但多遭失败。同其祖父成吉思汗一样，忽必烈是蒙古民族光辉历史的缔造者，是蒙古族卓越的政治家、军事家。他在位35年，1294年正月，在大都病逝，谥号圣德神功文武皇帝，庙号世祖。

前的史料和考古发掘中没有找到其在北京留下帝王陵寝的记录。

事实上，元世祖忽必烈定都北京也与金海陵王完颜亮一样历经考据。据《元史》记载，蒙古贵族巴图鲁曾对元世祖"说明"北京："幽燕之地，龙蟠虎踞，形势雄伟，南控江淮，北连朔漠，大王果欲经营天下，驻跸之所，非燕不可。"大臣刘秉忠也主张定都北京，忽必烈接受了他们的意见，于1264年定都北京。此后，元代以北京为大都，以"前朝后市，左祖右社"为原则建设，奠定了北京城的规模。然而，随着明朝的崛起，元大都和一个一度纵横捭阖的王朝一起消失在历史深处，也将一代代帝王百年后的身家秘密带到了后人的视野之外。金代的真龙天子埋伏于北京地下，元代的真龙天子或许早已云游他乡。

明 圣上龙兴之地 帝王万世之都

一三六八至一六四四

历经金、元两代，北京是风水宝地，既能成就霸业亦能在其后保佑皇帝雄踞天下已是不争的事实。因此，到了明朝奠定基业并在南京落脚，朱元璋的第四个儿子明成祖朱棣扫平障碍终于上位，他的群臣看出他无意在南京久留的"心事"，也开始为他谋划大明王朝的永居之地。

关于这次"论证"，有两个传说，都与射箭有关。南京人比较愿意相信的是"徐达箭射北京"。皇帝问群臣，何处定都最好，群臣推举膂力过人的徐达，一箭向北射出，箭落之处，便是国都。传说之所以能留传，很大程度上在于它神乎其神，且充满温厚的历史情怀。于是，很自然地，徐达的箭稳稳当当插在了北京城中心。北京人更倾向相信"箭落幽州"。传说在燕王扫北时，这位志存高远的未来皇帝已经开始顺便寻找日后的都城，是不是徐达射箭不重要，重要的是那位射箭的大将的箭尖究竟落在哪里。今天的河北赵县、安国市的百姓中老辈人都有被这一箭"戳中"的自豪感，他们更愿意相信，他们的故乡其实才是一代天骄明成祖最初选中或者天赐给人间龙子的宝地，进军北京是后来的顺势而为。

传说终归是传说，在《明实录·太宗实录》中记载的群臣上疏如下："伏惟北京，圣上龙兴之地，北枕居庸，西峙太行，东连山海，南俯中原，沃野千里，山川形势，足以控四夷，制天下，诚帝王万世之都也。"这应该算是负责任的论证，也正好符合了过往的金、元两代以及更早的文化典籍中对北京地理环境的界定和分析。事实上，直至近代，研究北京风物、地理、环境的学者也一致认为，综观北京地形，依山面海，腹地辽阔，形势雄伟。在山川襟带之间，北京城温润丰饶，土地肥沃，藏风聚气，拥有利于生态平衡和人类发展的最佳格局。

与金海陵王完颜亮一样，明成祖入主京城后即开始为自己百年之后寻觅安居之所，这几乎已经成为历朝历代皇帝必修的功课、必了的心事。用今天的观念来解释这份事死如事生的帝王情

怀，多少会有些无厘头，当人们无法确定死后灵魂何所去时，对身后事的关注便划分为两极，关注者则格外希望能在另一个世界安逸祥和，不关注者则越发全神贯注于当下。而对于那些坚定地认为自己是享尽人间荣华富贵的帝王真龙天命，他们无法不寄望于死后仍能在另一个世界继续过曾经的生活，维持曾经的尊贵。或许，这是世界上一切奢华陵墓诞生的初衷。明十三陵也不例外。

在今天北京昌平的天寿山南麓，分布着十三处明代帝王陵寝，方圆40平方公里的小盆地上，次第有长陵、献陵、景陵、

裕陵、茂陵、泰陵、康陵、永陵、昭陵、定陵、庆陵、德陵、思陵。另有因"夺门之变"而未能入葬祖坟的景泰帝朱祁镇的陵墓坐落于京西玉泉山脚下，后人称其为景泰陵。它与天寿山脚下的明十三陵一道构成目前中国保存最为完整的帝王墓葬群。

公元1368年朱元璋打败元代统治者建立明朝。建国后，继承历代汉族统治的传统，提倡儒学，以礼治国。明朝为帝王和文武官员制定出严格的墓葬规矩，朱元璋的孝陵建在南京，前有排列石人石兽的墓道，后有举行祭祀活动的恩殿。

殿后为墓穴上方的大土堆，筑成圆形城堡，称为"宝城"。在宝城前另建高大城台，城台上建筑城楼，称为"方城明楼"。这种布置奠定了明代皇陵的基本格式，也是北京明十三陵所遵从的格式。公元1409年，明成祖朱棣初到北京，即开始大规模兴建皇宫并为皇陵选址。明成祖最终选定了北京昌平境内的一处吉壤，改原名黄土山为定陵地宫，历时四年至永乐十一年（1413年）完成主体工程，并于同年葬入徐皇后。永乐二十二年（1424年），明成祖在北征回师途中病逝，迁徐皇后与之合葬入长陵。

作为世界瞩目的历史遗产，北京明十三陵的保护和研究从未停止。1950年，刚刚成立的新中国对明十三陵陵寝进行了及时的管护；1955年，北京市政府根据国务院的意见接管明十三陵，并于当年派出建筑队对长陵、景陵、永陵进行修缮；1957年，北京市政府公布十三陵为北京市第一批重点古建文物保护单位；1961年，十三陵被公布为全国重点文物保护单位；1981年6月，在十三陵特区办事处成立之后，通过"以文养文"的方式，将大量旅游收入投入陵寝的修缮工作中，德陵、康陵、庆陵、泰陵先后不同程度地进行了修整；1982年，国务院公布"八达岭——十三陵风景区"为全国44个重点风景名胜保护区之一；1991年，十三陵被国家旅游局确定为"中国旅游胜地四十佳"之一；1992年，十三陵被北京旅游世界之最评选委员会评为"世界上保存完整埋葬皇帝最多的墓葬群"；2003年，明十三陵被世界教科文组织确定为"世界文化遗产"。其中最后两个自清乾隆年间以来再未修缮过的裕陵和茂陵也于近年进行了修缮。

1956年至1958年，考古工作者对定陵地下玄宫进行发掘，出土了大量珍贵的文物。此后几十年间，其他陵墓一直没有进行同等规模的开掘，包括号称中国考古第一人的夏鼐教授也力主在科技水平尚不足以确保文物安全的情况下，"暂缓发掘"。随之而来的是民间对帝王陵墓中各种机关、悬疑的无尽猜想和附会，更多的秘密保留在巨大恢弘的墓葬群落中。著名古建筑专家罗哲文评价说："明十三陵建筑价值极高，长陵的楠木殿其规模是全国唯一的，石雕精湛。明十三陵无论是从建筑形式，还是建筑结构，或建筑艺术上看，是明代建筑的实物历史。"

塔林之春、献陵瑞雪、神路通天、长陵秋色……这些人们熟悉的明十三陵美景至今仍年年岁岁点缀着古老的北京。据说，天寿山是京城龙脉所在，而沉睡在地下城池中头枕龙脉的明代"真龙天子"也像他们生前所希望的那样，与北京这片厚土相濡以沫，永不分离。

清 龙穴砂水形势理气诸吉咸备

一六一六至一九一一

汉文化的力量究竟有多强大？很多学者喜欢以元朝和清朝的政治、经济、文化发展举例说明。回到龙与地下城这个主题，则有充足的史料能证实明十三陵在建造陵寝方面对清朝的帝王们形成的强大而不可抗拒的影响。

清朝的两位开国皇帝清太祖努尔哈赤和清太宗皇太极在世时，全国尚未统一，他们已经认识到，满族若不吸取汉族的先进文化和统治经验，则无法统一天下并维护封建统治。于是，他们召用明朝的降臣并委以重任，细心学习明朝的各种制度和法律。公元1644年，顺治皇帝入关，全面继承明制，使用紫禁城全部建筑，同时，在陵墓建筑上学习明皇陵的经验。传说他在某次游猎时亲自在北京东郊燕山之下选定陵址，建造孝陵。之后，顺治皇后的孝东陵、康熙的景陵相继建成，形成陵区，便是今天位于河北省遵化市的清东陵。可以说东陵完全模仿了明十三陵，各陵既独立又有统一规划。现在的东陵包括顺治的孝陵、康熙的景陵、乾隆的裕陵、咸丰的定陵、同治的惠陵，以及东（慈安）、西（慈禧）太后等后陵四座、妃园寝五座、公主陵一座，一共埋葬14位皇后和136位妃嫔。

在中国历史上关于谋朝篡位、皇室之内父子手足相残的权谋故事举不胜举，清朝的雍正皇帝也"有幸"加入其中。雍正篡改父亲康熙皇帝的遗诏靠耍手段谋得帝位是传奇故事最喜欢使用的素材，因此，人们顺理成章地解释了在已拥有清东陵如此大规模的帝王陵墓群之后，雍正皇帝因为不想和父亲葬在一处，不想死后还要对父亲谢罪听其训斥，改变了父子同葬的祖制，在今天河北省易县大兴土

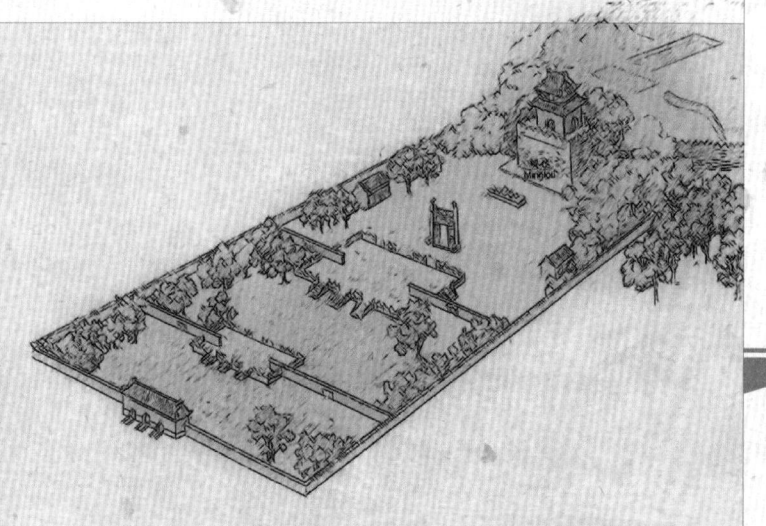

木建造清西陵。事实上，清西陵有极好的成为皇帝陵寝的"条件"。清代孙鼎烈在《永宁山扈从纪程》中这样描述西陵："山势自太行来，巍峨耸拔，脉秀力丰，峻岭崇岗，远拱于外，灵岩翠岫，环卫其间。"这里被誉为"华北地区最大的古松林"，8000余公顷土地上20000多株古松屹立，在这里兴建"帝王谷"堪称"乾坤聚秀之区、阴阳合汇之所"，很难说身边"高人"无数的雍正皇帝不是看中了这块宝地的山川形势。清西陵有帝陵4座，雍正的泰陵、嘉庆的昌陵、道光的慕陵和光绪的崇陵。后陵3座，即泰东陵、昌西陵、慕东陵。妃陵3座，即泰妃陵、昌妃陵、崇妃陵。此外，还有公主陵、阿哥陵、王爷陵等一共14座。1995年，末代皇帝溥仪的骨灰历经辗转葬入清西陵，至此，一个王朝皇室之内的生生死死画上了句号。

在中国的帝王陵墓中，无论明十三陵还是清东陵和西陵，都按照帝王们死后仍为九五之尊的愿望，复制了他们生前生活的宫廷形制。在另一个世界中，他们继续着人中之王、真命天子的千秋大梦。

无论清朝自1644年入关到1911年被推翻这段历程中究竟有多少烟云往事、热血传奇，有一位女子绝对不能忽视，她便是两

朝听政、权倾天下的慈禧太后。按照清朝祖制，皇后于皇帝去世后辞世，应建造后陵于帝陵左右，但规模必须比帝陵小。然而对于一生致力于"女性革命"和"女性执政"甚至"女性独裁"的慈禧太后，祖制根本不适用于她。她的陵墓在清代的一切皇家陵寝中占据了建筑精美、耗资巨大、陪葬奢华等数个第一，当然，她也是第一位在死后20年即"见识"了炸药的皇室成员。

慈禧太后的陵墓之豪华，超过紫禁城，其陪葬品之价值难以估量。陪伴她走到最后的大太监李莲英在《爱月轩笔记》中记载："慈禧尸体入棺前，先在棺底铺三层金丝串珠锦褥和一层珍珠，厚一尺；头部上首为翠荷叶，脚下置粉红碧玺莲花；头戴珍珠凤冠，冠上最大一颗珍珠大如鸡卵，价值1000万两白银；身旁放金、宝石、玉、翠雕佛爷27尊；脚下两边各放翡翠西瓜、甜瓜、白菜，还有宝石制成的桃、李、杏、枣200多枚；身左放玉石莲花，身右放玉雕珊瑚树；另外还有玉石骏马8尊，玉石十八罗汉，共计700多件。葬殓完毕，又倒入4升珍珠、宝石

2200块填棺。"这种百年之后仍富甲天下的连城之财，在1928年被军阀孙殿英率部将陵墓爆破后洗劫一空，至今，被盗窃的文物珍宝大部分不知所终。

　　如果用今天的眼光来看，慈禧太后颇有"个性"。她的陵墓设计曾三易其稿，三度重建。也正是因为她的所谓"贪得无厌""穷奢极欲"，才为后人留下了如此精美的建筑文化遗产。在她的陵墓中，恩殿及左右配殿的梁柱门窗全部用黄花梨木和楠木制成，木梁柱上以金粉绘制龙、凤、云、寿图案。在三座殿的里外彩画中，金色的龙有2400多条，至今仍金光闪烁。在三座殿的三面墙上镶有30块不同大小的雕花砖壁，砌出"五蝠捧寿"和"字不到头"图案，象征福寿吉祥。恩殿台基栏杆上雕满龙凤纹样，周围69块栏板的两面共138副"凤引龙追"图案；栏杆上的74根柱头上，全部是凤凰穿云的雕刻，而在柱身上则雕有升龙出水。就像电影《垂帘听政》中所表现的那样，在慈禧太后还只是少女玉兰时已经"志存高远"："为什么不能凤在上、龙在下？"如今慈禧陵墓中的这些精雕细琢的"遗产"默默地告诉人们，她是清朝276年历史、12位皇帝、数以万计的嫔妃中真正得遂凌云之志的奇才，女性之光照亮了大清的最后时光。

　　北京有独特的厚土，滋生和养育着独特的文化，这是一座卧虎藏龙的城市，也是一座诞生奇迹的城市。即使在不经意的行走中，也有可能遇见一处古迹，遇见一段传说，随后，也有可能，撞破了埋藏在860余年都城史任意一个节点上的某个秘密，也许，沿着这个秘密走下去，便能遇见北京特色的龙与地下城。

北京城紀

章节·叁

至尊 豪杰之所

那是一种玩具，与其他带有本土特色的玩具不同的是，它风靡世界。它是塑料积木，靠小朋友动脑动手，拼插出变化无穷的造型。它叫乐高，1932年诞生于丹麦。作为超级乐高控，6岁女孩宝宝最爱的是乐高与建筑大师合作的世界著名建筑系列。拥有了乐高版古根海姆博物馆等一系列经典建筑玩具的她，决定在最近给乐高总部写一封信，"希望他们认真考虑做一套北京建筑"，因为"北京什么都有"，而最酷的是，在北京860余年的建都史上，先后有42名皇帝在这里执掌江山。

中国人把皇帝的椅子称为"龙椅"，自金代迁都北京始，至中国封建社会最后一名皇帝退位，北京这片豪杰之所安置着42名皇帝的龙椅，堪称至尊之地。而这42人来自女真族、蒙古族、汉族和满族这四个民族，他们率领着他们的子民在北京开疆拓土、安居乐业、发展经济、滋养文化，让这里渐渐成为一座融合中华各民族文明精华的包容的城市。

燕都的热土或许适宜栽种莲花

一一五至一二三四

城市和人一样，有命运的轨迹。北京开启建都史之初，很难说是不是恰好将自己的命运附会于一代枭雄。

1149年，金太祖完颜阿骨打的孙子，28岁的完颜亮弑杀金熙宗完颜亶夺取皇位，开始了他仅仅12年的帝王生涯。完颜亮史称海陵王，在民间文学和乡村野史中，他是嗜杀成性、骄奢淫逸的暴君。仅关于他杀害堂兄夺取皇位之际所杀人口数便有300余人、200余人、150余人等不同说法，极言其杀人不眨眼。一个靠杀人上位的君王，坐上被自己亲手杀害的堂兄的龙椅，心里多少会有些不安吧？海陵王完颜亮此时在已经立国34年的强大金国的国都上京会宁府（今黑龙江阿城）决计不能高枕无忧，而是时时要提防宗室贵族发动宫廷政变。这样，便有了流传至今的有关海陵王迁都北京的故事。"一日宴会间，海陵王问右丞相梁汉臣：'朕栽莲二百本而俱死，何也？'梁汉臣答曰：'自古江南为桔，江北为枳，非种者不能，盖地势然也。上都地寒，惟燕京地暖，可栽莲。'于是海陵王诏曰：'依卿所请，择日而迁。'"

《金史》中记载的海陵王完颜亮是一名极有韬略、胸怀大志且深谙汉文化精髓并精于立法治国的超级政治人才。以他的深谋远虑，迁都的事情绝不会如此草率随性。事实上，当时

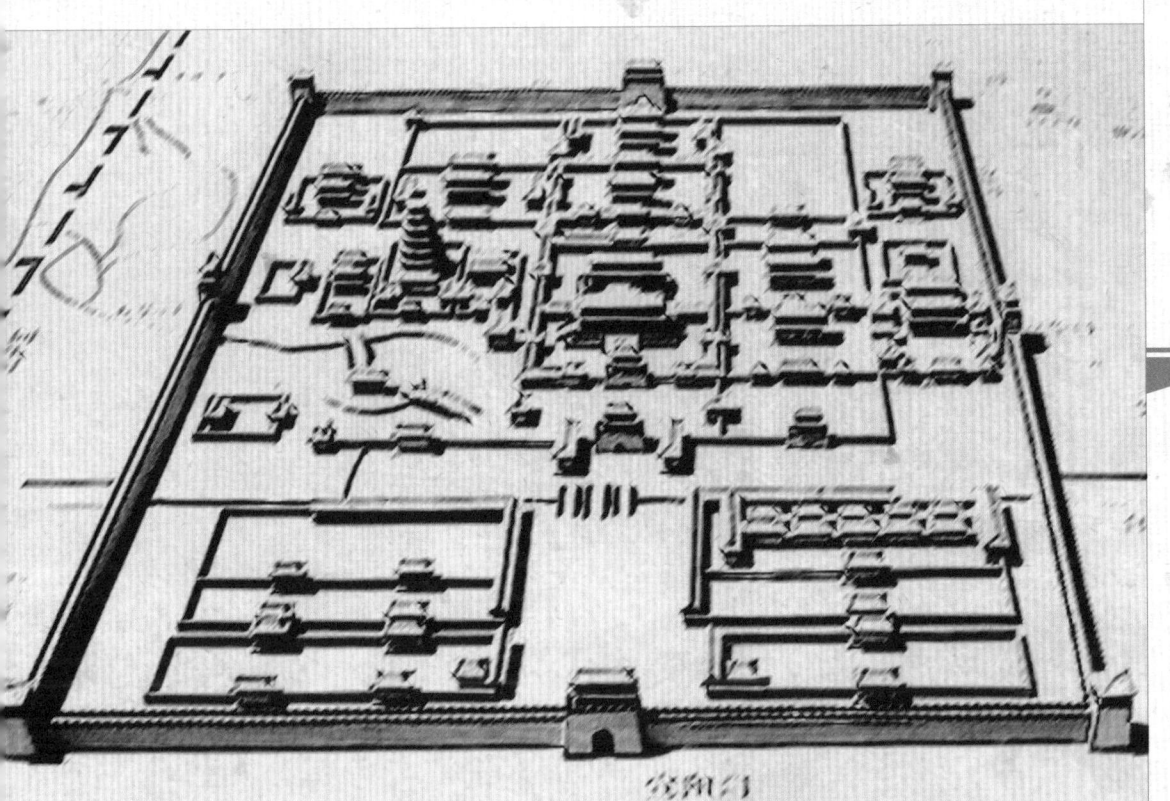

的上京会宁府偏于一隅,"供馈困于转输,使命苦于驿顿",国都地处金国极北,难于有效辖控中原大地,"方疆广于万里,以北则民清而事简,以南则地远而事繁",南方的粮食、布匹不能及时供达,且要在运送途中蒙受巨大耗费。而此时早已被灭掉的辽国留下的燕京宫室仍基本保存,无论在地理、经济乃至规模和形制上,都无疑具备成为最好的新国都的条件。

于是,北京,在1153年,迎来了命运的转机和第一位真正在此号令天下的皇帝,掀开了辉煌的都城史。

金朝坐镇北京即金中都的皇帝共7位,自海陵王完颜亮起至1234年即位仅一天便死于乱军之中成为亡国之君的金昭宗完颜承麟止，金朝结束了在北京坐中央之地而号令天下的历史。无论对海陵王完颜亮的历史评价如何毁誉参半，至少，在建设北京这一点上，他劳苦功高。金中都可以说是在当时历史条件下的"集大成之作"。参与的设计和监工者以及施工者中，有汉人，也有渤海人乃至当时聚居燕京的少数民族工匠，他们把不同民族的民族文化融入中都的建筑之中。海陵王本身仰慕汉文化，并极力促成女真人的汉化，因此，金中都宫室总体设计仿照北宋都城汴京制度。在修建之前，海陵王"遣画工写京师（指汴京）宫室制度，至于阔狭修短，曲尽其数，授之左相张浩辈，按图以修之"。因此，金中都宫城布局甚至名称多有与汴京相同或近似之处，宫殿的主要殿堂所呈的"工"字形就是汴京的建筑形式。海陵王修金中都时，还把汴京宫殿中的某些构件拆卸下来直接用于中都宫殿建筑，甚

至将北宋宫里的摆件、饰物移置中都宫中。自海陵王迁都筑成金中都后，经过60年不间断的营建修缮，"宫阙雄丽，为古今冠"。

海陵王还是一位极有才华的文学家、诗人，金代皇帝的汉文化水平都相当高，但就诗词的成就而言，以他为最。他的诗词雄浑遒劲，气象恢弘，充满了不为人下的雄霸之气。他曾写下"万里车书一混同，江南岂有别疆封？提兵百万西湖上，立马吴山第一峰"的诗句，极尽豪杰霸气，志在"天下一家"。尽管时至今日，金中都在北京所剩遗迹并不多，但海陵王的迁都，开启了北京作为此后历朝历代国都的新纪元，功在千秋。

元 黄金之城住不下征伐不息的灵魂

一二七一至一三六八

"不论大汗坐在哪一殿堂之上,总要依照一定的惯例。他的桌子安放得比别人的高出一大截。他坐的位置是在大厅的北端,面孔朝南,他的正妻坐在左首。右侧坐着他的儿子和侄儿们,在座的也有其他皇室成员。这些人只是坐得更低,低到他们的头与大汗的脚处于同一水平线上。其他一些王侯们坐在更低一些的桌子旁。大汗的侄儿们的夫人和其他一些女眷坐在大汗右侧较低的桌旁,再下面便是王侯武士们的女眷,每人都坐在大汗为他们指定的位置。这样设置桌子,是为了皇上能够看到所有的在座者,看到每个人……"写下这段话的人号称曾亲自拜会了元世祖忽必烈,并在他缔造的大都即今天的北京过了一段被奉为上宾的舒服日子。他是意大利人马可·波罗,到达元大都时,年方二十出头,游历了元朝的大好河山之后回到他的国家,写下了一本至今仍在东西方世界流传却也饱受质疑的《马可·波罗游记》。曾经,西方人了解神秘的东方和号称中国恺撒的忽必烈,就靠这本书。

在今天的北京元大都遗址公园，忽必烈的坐像庄严而充满霸气。他仿佛仍在俯视曾代表着帝国辉煌的都城，踌躇满志。事实上，在他之前，中国的版图从未有过那样辽阔，中国的战士们也从未有过那样长的征途。史书记载元朝的"战绩"和疆土："起朔漠，并西域，平西夏，灭女真，臣高丽，定南诏，遂下江南，而天下为一，故其地北逾阴山，西极流沙，东尽辽左，南越海表。盖汉东西九千三百二里，南北一万三千三百六十八里，唐东西九千五百一十一里，南北一万六千九百一十八里，元东南所至不下汉、唐，而西北则过之，有难以里数限者矣。"

1206年成吉思汗建国，以族名为国名，称大蒙古国；忽必烈称汗后，建年号"中统"，并未另立国名。1271年11月，在建国十多年之后，他的统治地位已逐渐巩固，才正式建国号"大元"，下诏说："顷者耆宿（指子聪等）诣庭，奏章申请，谓既成于大业，宜早定于鸿名"，"可建国号曰大元，盖取《易经》'大哉乾元'之义"。这个"大元"已不仅仅属于蒙古民族，而是中原封建王朝的继续。1272年二月，忽必烈采纳他宠信的汉臣刘秉忠的建议，改中都为大都，宣布在此建都。1273年，大都宫殿建成。次年正月，忽必烈在元大都皇城正殿接受朝贺。元朝15位大汗君主，定居北京并在此履帝王生涯者，自忽必烈始，至最后

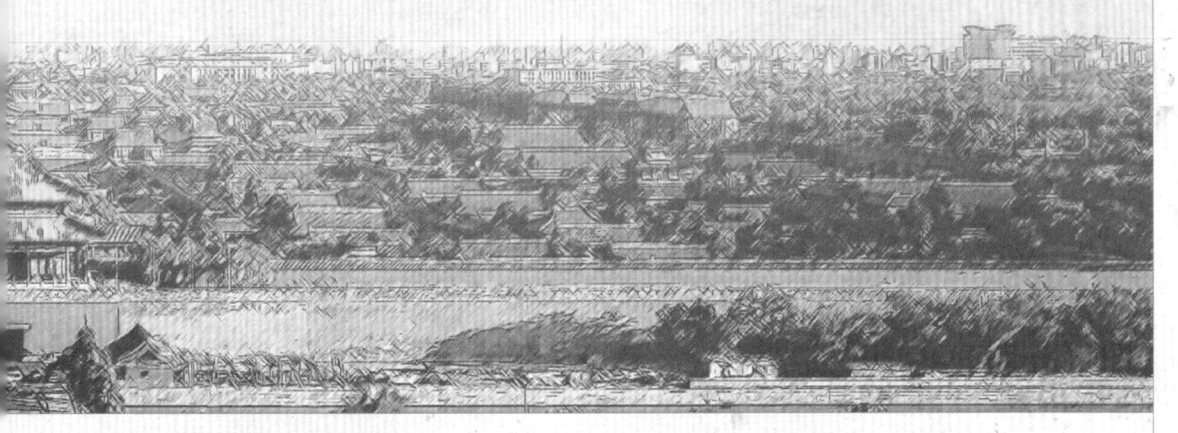

一位元顺帝终，共11人。赶走了女真人的蒙古族统治者为北京带来了又一次民族融合和政治、经济、文化的空前繁荣。

建筑学家梁思成在《伟大的中轴线》中写道："一根长达八公里，全世界最长，也最伟大的南北中轴线穿过了全城。北京独有的壮美秩序就由这条中轴的建立而产生……有这样气魄的建筑总布局，以这样规模来处理空间，世界上就没有第二个！"北京的中轴线发轫于金朝，彼时已小有规模，但真正成为梁思成所描述的这样，成为日后北京建筑格局规划的强有力依据，始于忽必烈兴建元大都。可以说，在北京精彩的建筑史上，忽必烈是不容忽视的一位起到关键作用的君王。

忽必烈在位35年，其间他将大都打造成为一座名副其实的国际化城市。从城市建筑的角度来说，元大都的拥有者忽必烈是蒙古人，总设计师刘秉忠是汉族人，总工程师也黑迭儿是阿拉伯人……其时元大都城中有许多"色目人"即阿拉伯人，有些还是高官富商，他们带来了西亚的建筑类型和形式，融合到大都的建设当中。同时，在城市经济、贸易和商业的发展方面，大都也是一派国际大都市的热闹景象。还是马可·波罗，他以"驻大都记者"的腔调描述当时所见："每个城郊在距城墙约一英里的地方建有旅馆或招待骆驼商队的大旅店，可提供各地往来商人的居住之所，并且不同的人都住在不同的指定的住所，而这些住所又是相互隔开的。例如一种住所指定给伦巴人，另一种指定给德意志人，第三种指定给法兰西人……每当有外国专使来到大都，如果他们负有与大汗利益相关的任务，则他们照例是由皇家招待的。"可见当时大都与欧亚其他国家的商务和外交往来之频繁。同时，大都在马可·波罗笔下也是全世界的特产与物流的中心，凡是世界各地最稀奇最有价值的东西都会集中在这个城市，印度的宝石、珍珠、药材和香料，契丹各省和帝国其他地方丰饶的物产供商人们在这里转卖，来自南方的金丝织物和绫罗绸缎出售于都城内的商铺……这种物产、文化乃至人流的融合，在忽必烈的元大都蔚为壮观，在北京的城邦历史上也成为一道传奇风景。

忽必烈虽不像辽太祖耶律阿保机那样"能汉语"，但对汉文化、汉族知识精英非常看重。他倚重汉族重臣，也推崇历史上历代沿革的汉家皇朝的治国之道。他推动了蒙古族新的文字诞生，这种新型文字因其更加与时俱进而得以实现与其他各民族文字特别是汉语的互译和交流，促进了大中国的民族融合。

人们常说，君主是人而不是神，文韬武略、胸怀博大如忽必烈，仍有一颗感性的心。尽管坐拥天下，忽必烈的晚年并不幸福，他先是失去了贴心的皇后察必，随后，他的继承人皇子真金英年早逝，在个人生活纷乱如麻的时候，他部署的一系列远征遭遇挫折，在日本、在海上、在南亚，他的军队不断受挫。年近80岁时，忽必烈又一次披挂上阵亲征进犯和林的蒙古宗王海都，这一次，他已疲惫的身心遭受了前所未有的打击。

忽必烈卒于80岁，一世英豪。曾经，1283年，忽必烈下令在菜市口刑场（今北京宣武门外）处死南宋宰相文天祥，因为担心大都人引火烧城，特意将各处城垣、屋顶的草席撤下。然而到了1368年元朝末代皇帝元顺帝的最后时光，明朝开国皇帝朱元璋的军队一举烧毁了元大都，这座曾经的黄金之城终于荡然无存，而此时忽必烈永在征途的灵魂唯有随着他被逐出大都的后代重返故乡蒙古草原。

明 热血英雄被供奉得久了也便成为神

一三六八至一六四四

元朝灭亡的一场大火结束了这个强大帝国在北京的统治，徐达和常遇春骁勇无敌剑指北方，奠定了大明朝北上定国的基业。1368年初，出身布衣的明太祖朱元璋在应天即今天的南京登基，国号大明，开始了长达276年的明朝政权。明朝是中国历史上承元朝、下启清朝的朝代，是以汉族为主推翻蒙古族统治者而建立起来的汉族复兴王朝，也是中国历史上最后一个由汉族建立的君主制王朝。

明朝16位皇帝，自明成祖朱棣迁都北京至明思宗崇祯皇帝自缢于北京景山，14位皇帝与北京结下不解之缘。明朝历经盛世而后逐渐衰微，其迤逦而来的路程与北京的城市建筑史紧密相关。直至今日，紫禁城、天坛、太庙、历代帝王庙等北京的地标性建筑尽皆出于明朝，北京成为象征封建王权、体现中国帝王九五之尊的天命之地、灵杰之所，并为后人留下宝贵的建筑文化、历史文化遗产，其集大成并磅礴发展，也在明朝。

1403年，明成祖朱棣登基称永乐皇帝的元年，皇帝诏以北平为北京，改北平府为顺天府。自此，开始了长达18年的北京皇家宫殿建设，同时修会通河、疏浚运河，以保粮草银钱贸易的南北畅通。永乐十九年即1421年，朱棣在北京御奉天殿，朝百官，大祀南郊。至此，明朝的迁都大政基本完成。

梁启超在《祖国大航海家郑和传》中对明成祖朱棣有极高

的评价:"成祖以雄才大略,承高帝之后,天下初定,国力大充,乃思扬威德于域外,此其与汉孝武、唐太宗之时代正相类。成祖既北定鞑靼,耀兵于乌梁海以西,西辟乌斯藏,以法号羁縻其酋,南戡越南,夷为郡县。陆运之盛,几追汉唐,乃更进而树威于新国。郑和之业,其主动者,实绝世英主明成祖其人也。"明成祖堪为人中龙凤,他在位期间可谓盛世,留下了至今令中国人感喟自豪的两大政绩。其一为命解缙、姚广孝、王景、邹辑等人纂修《永乐大典》,这是中国古代编纂的一部大型类书,收录入《永乐大典》的图书均未删未改,是中国古代最大的百科全书,也是当时世界上最大的百科全书,比18世纪中叶出版的《大英百科全书》和《法国百科全书》要早300多年。其二为建造紫禁城。北京紫禁城筹建于明永乐五年(1407年),兴建于永乐十五年至十八年。整个营造工程由侯爵陈圭督造,具体负责者是规划师吴中。从1407年起,明成祖集中全国匠师,征调了二三十万民工和军工,经过14年的时间,建成了这组规模宏大的宫殿组群,成为世界历史上最著名的建筑之一。紫禁城经历了此后的风云变幻,至今,仍保存明代遗风。

　　盛世之下,修宗祠、建宗庙是历代皇帝的心愿。时至今日,北京流传着"有桥没有水,有碑没有驮,有钟没有鼓,有庙没有佛"的民谚,这个神奇所在,便是位于今天北京西城区阜成门内大街路北、修建于明朝嘉靖九年(1530年)的历代帝王庙。历代帝王庙是目前中国唯一保存完整的祭祀历代帝王的皇家坛庙,其地位与太庙和孔庙相齐,成为皇帝亲自祭祀的京城三大皇家大庙宇之一。按照嘉靖皇帝修建帝王庙的意愿,这里供奉着中国自三皇五帝以来的历代皇帝和或参与开国或辅佐守业的历代先贤。而自嘉靖修建完成历代帝王庙至清末的380年间，在这里至少举行过662次祭祀大典。

中国的皇帝不是神，无论他们来自哪个民族、胸怀何种治国安邦的理念，大都有一个共同点——他们是华夏民族的精英分子，是中国漫漫历史长河中的"法施于民""以死勤事""以劳定国""能御大灾""能捍大患"的英雄豪杰，值得后世追思、景仰。也正基于此，历代帝王庙中那些被供奉的先君前贤，久而久之成了中国历史中被神化的一个独特人群。

明朝的皇帝中有明太祖朱元璋这样在民间被传诵的"乞丐皇帝"，也有明成祖朱棣这样功高盖世却被后世诟病为残暴的毁誉参半的传奇人物，更有修建了历代帝王庙这样的华夏宗祠自己却痴迷于宗教甚至热衷炼丹术数的嘉靖皇帝，而14位君主中的最后一位，明思宗崇祯皇帝，在北京坐皇位17年，其"下场"最为惨烈。

北京人说起崇祯皇帝，总会提到煤山（现北京景山公园）的歪脖树。历经以讹传讹，也历经考证，至今，关于崇祯皇帝的自缢处仍存有各种争议。崇祯是明朝的亡国之君，待到他登基即位，明朝已苟延残喘。如果说中国的帝王总是敢为天下先，那么在对全体国民谢罪这一点上，无人能出崇祯其右。这位辞世时年仅35岁的末代国君曾六次对自己的臣民下"罪己诏"，检讨身为一国之君的无能和羞愤。崇祯在位期间，天下已成大乱之势，农民起义此起彼伏，清军在关外"叫嚣"不止，天灾人祸层出不穷。崇祯十七年即1644年，也是这位国破家亡的青年君主最后一次对天下人谢罪，他的"罪己诏"成为他的临终遗言。此时，李自成的农民起义军已兵临城下，绝望无助的崇祯举行了最后一次家宴，宴罢，即安排太子慈烺、三子定王慈炯、四子永王慈焕逃离皇宫。随后，他在宫中亲自持剑砍杀妻妾、女儿，一生贤德的周皇后于坤宁宫自缢。次日凌晨，崇祯带着御笔太监王承恩离开紫禁城，登上皇家禁苑煤山即今天的景山，在一株老槐树下自缢身亡。死时"以发覆面，白夹蓝袍白细裤，一足跣，一足有绫袜"，衣上以血指书。崇祯皇帝在遗言中写道："朕自登极十七年，虽朕薄德匪躬，上干天怒，致逆贼直逼京师，然皆诸臣之误朕也，朕死，无面目见祖宗于地下，自去冠冕，以发覆面，任贼分裂朕尸，勿伤百姓一人。"

公元1644年农历三月十九日这一天，在中国历史上也是大明王朝的亡国祭日，自此，又一个王朝的背影在北京这片土地上渐行渐远。

清 伤城之内满园深浅色总是旧河山
一六一六至一九一一

一条贯穿北京的中轴线将这座城市清晰地"规制"起来，前朝后市、左祖右社、坛台四环。中国典籍《吕氏春秋》中有言："于天下之中而立国，于国之中而立宫，于宫之中而立庙"，这也是北京作为几代都城营建的原则。北京的中轴线，被尊为王者之轴，或许也包含着沿此轴线上行至九重宫殿觐见皇帝之意。传说，有一位外国使节到访清廷，不肯跪拜皇帝，于是，聪明的礼部官员引领这位"只跪上帝、不跪国君"的西方外交官自正阳门沿中轴线北上，一路经过大清门、千步廊和御道，让他"瞻仰"了金色的天安门、朱砂色的城楼、洁白的阶石栏杆、高耸的石狮华表，走过端门、午门，直至太和殿广场，辽阔肃穆、威武庄严的东方皇家气派令他在太和殿上身不由己地跪倒……散落于民间的故事见证着曾经大清帝国的威仪。

历史从来都有其自身发展的规律，1911年辛亥革命之前，北京这座城市的命运线和历代帝王的命运线充满吊诡地相辅相成。中国最后一个王朝大清帝国自14岁亲政的顺治皇帝起至末代皇帝溥仪颁布《退位诏书》止，在北京的紫禁城内安放了10把龙椅。

和其他朝代一样，清朝在200多年的统治中有过辉煌的太平盛世，例如人们耳熟能详的康乾盛世。和之前的金朝女真族皇帝、元朝蒙古族皇帝一样，清朝的皇帝们极为推崇汉文化，并且积极促进华夏各民族文化的融合。与前朝历代不同的是，清朝时的中国已极为开放，北京常年有盘桓于此的欧洲人、西亚人、印度人、阿拉伯人，商旅、传教士、艺术家、淘金者，无所不包。清朝入关后的第一位皇帝顺治在争取汉人地主、提高汉官权力、重用汉官方面，进行了大胆的尝试和努力，同时他也是一位积极学习汉族文化的勤勉的"学生"。更为"国际化"的是，顺治皇帝遇见了来自德意志的传教士汤若望，尊其为"玛法"即汉族所称爷爷，向汤若望请教有关天文历算、社会人生等各种问题。汤若望在顺治皇帝的心目中威信最高，顺治对他几乎言听计从，包括在逝世前立三子玄烨为皇太子以继承帝位，也是采纳汤若望的建议。如果说清朝时中国自上而下接受西方的科技文化并开始研习，顺治皇帝大概算是得风气之先。

顺治之后的中国，迎来了相当长时间的安定，康熙、雍正至乾隆三位皇帝，也为北京这座城市带来了在清朝这一时间轴上的最好时光。

清朝沿用明紫禁城，继续沿着中轴线完成进一步的城市规划。颇具创见的建设发生在乾隆皇帝在位期间。尽管彼时为帝国盛世，交通仍不发达。皇帝若想了解民间疾苦、倾听子民心声唯有走出深宫亲赴民间。乾隆一生六下江南，一面微服私访、察看吏治，一面饱览中国南方的优美山水和精致园林，并萌生了将天下园林齐聚京师的愿望。

乾隆皇帝在位60年，这期间他对北京的建设从未停止。他首先将始建于雍正时期的圆明园二十八景扩建为四十景，随后在其东边修建长春园，在香山修建静宜园，建成二十八景；1749年为向母亲祝寿，在瓮山兴建清漪园，即今天的万寿山和颐和园；同一时期对太后居住的畅春园进行大修，在其西部增建西花园，为皇子读书居住之所；又扩建玉泉山静明园，将玉泉山全部圈占，并修建静明园十六景。1760年，长春园北部西洋楼景区竣工。1769年，将圆明园东南若干皇子和公主赐园收回，并为绮春园。从此，北京最经典的园林建设工程全部完成。乾隆为北京留下了数十处建筑奇观，如天坛祈年殿蓝色琉璃瓦顶、颐和园、圆明园三园、香山、玉泉山等，这些皇家园林，体现着清代园林文化的辉煌。

变故总以钢铁节奏纷至沓来。乾隆皇帝的园林山水仍年年岁岁满园深浅色鲜花次第开，清帝国则被历史的巨手推到了覆灭的边缘，并最终以末代皇帝溥仪退位而告终。1912年退位时，溥仪年仅6岁，由隆裕皇后代为下诏，其诏书中写道："今全国人民心理，多倾向共和。南中各省，既倡义于前，北方诸将，亦主张于后。人心所向，天命可知。予亦何忍因一姓之尊荣，拂兆民之好恶。是用外观大势，内审舆情，特率皇帝将统治权公诸全国，定为共和立宪国体。近慰海内厌乱望治之心，远协古圣天下为公之义。"而溥仪的英国老师庄士敦在他的回忆录《紫禁城的黄昏》中记录了末代皇帝和平退位时与民国政府达成的条件，诸如皇帝辞位后，尊号仍存不废，岁用四百万元由中华民国拨用；暂居紫禁城，日后移居颐和园，侍卫人等照常留用等。至此，从顺治帝入主中原起延续了268年的清朝统治宣告结束。

作为皇帝，溥仪命运多舛，但是，在庄士敦的记录中，退位却是他为过上从帝王到平民的安逸生活而努力的开始。《紫禁城的黄昏》的尾声中有一段耐人寻味的描述："这些日子里，除了对外国的外交官们做一些回访之外，皇上从不走出使馆一

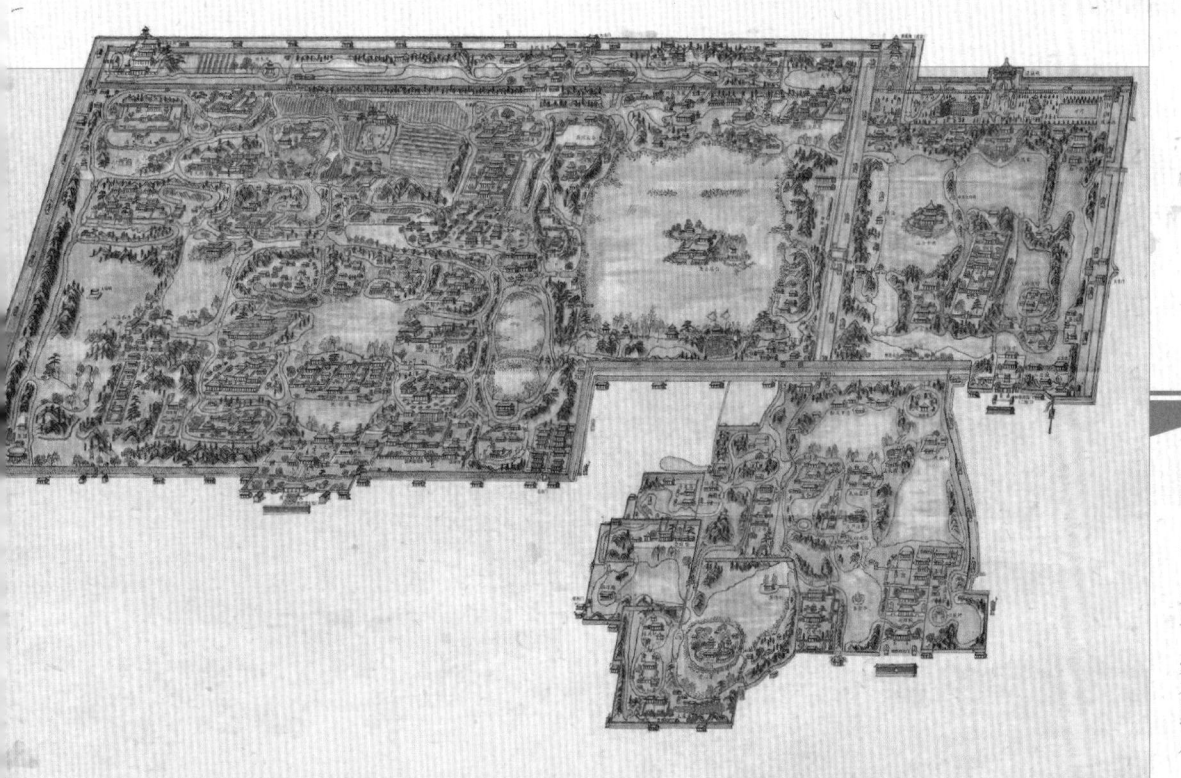

步。他只是经常到我在英国使馆的住处来。我们偶尔也一起爬到使馆区南边的那一小段城墙上散步,这里在中国人的管辖之外。站在这段城墙上,他第一次看到那绿荫环绕的天坛,巨大的白色大理石祭坛隐在树后。如果国运昌盛些,他将作为天子和人民之父在那里主持祭祀。站在这段城墙上,他还看见了紫禁城闪烁的黄色的琉璃瓦顶。从某些角度而言,他也许曾把那里看成是一座监狱,但那里必定是他从小居住的家……"

历经四个朝代贵为中国封建王朝都城的北京,是这些曾以刀光血影书写城市发展史的各族豪杰们的中兴之地,也是他们当中大部分人最终与时间同沉的安息之所。而他们留下的融汇华夏各民族文化特征的城市标识,都在讲述着860余年建都史上耀眼的故事。现在的北京,以包容的态度接纳时时刻刻扑面而来的一切,这是从她成为都城的第一天起便身体力行的城市精神。

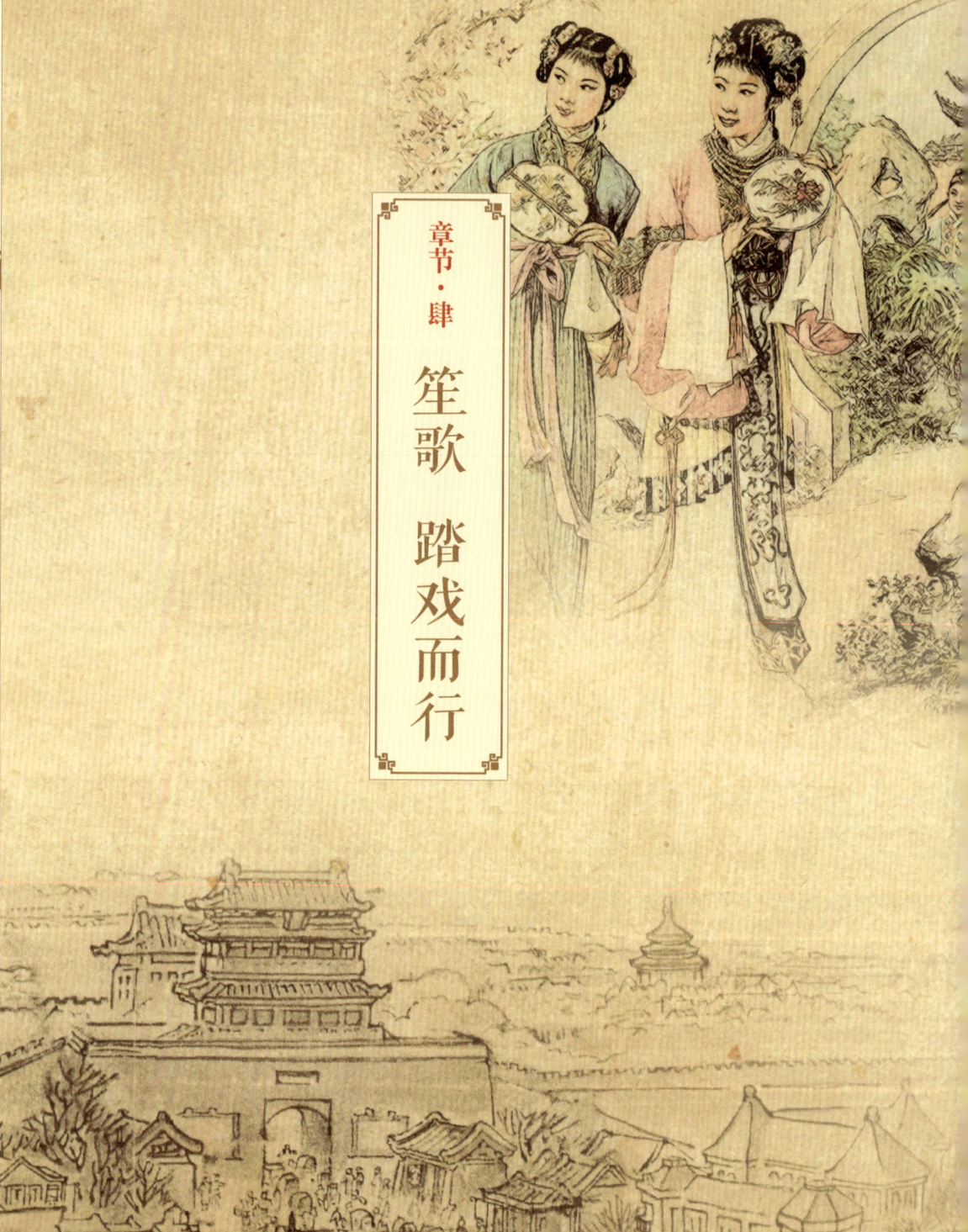

章节·肆

笙歌 踏戏而行

其实那里是一座监狱。安迪锁住狱警，独自"霸占"了专门用于对囚犯发号施令的房间。他放好一张唱片，将留声机对着扩音器，于是，普契尼的歌剧响彻监狱的上空。看过电影《肖申克的救赎》的观众，一定会记得这一段。"那是一个自由的时刻，因此多年以后，作为演员，还会对这段情节记忆犹新。"男主角安迪的扮演者蒂姆·罗宾斯在这部电影上映10年后的2005年仍陶醉地说。

时光回到1815年，一代枭雄拿破仑在滑铁卢大势已去，被囚禁于圣赫勒拿岛上。他有6年的时间可以回顾自己大半生的际遇和奋斗。信史之外的故事中说，拿破仑曾深深怀念在巴黎聆听享有盛名的歌剧时的尊贵和悠闲。那令他流连的记忆和挥之不去的声音，其中或许深藏着原本可以平静走完一辈子的玄机。

有时候，历史是牢笼，将曾经的波诡云谲、风云际会封闭在多少年后今人可见、可触的史料和遗存之中。时间连成线，空间则需要后来者一砖一瓦搭建起来，唯其如此才有可能实现所谓穿越历史的时空——人的心有多大，这条时空的管道则会有多宽，其间有纵横捭阖的热血英雄纷至沓来，也有历朝历代的风花雪月、歌舞升平。在厚重的史实之上，有一种声音，悬浮、飘荡、绵延至今，后来者姑且称之为笙歌。抚摸其如丝如缕不绝于耳的纤细脉络，探究其背后伶人舞台上演绎的悲欢离合，这一切坐实在一座城市的古往今来之内，则依稀可以看到，无论不同王朝的生逢盛世还是遭遇崎岖，城池与人，每每踏戏而行。

有着860余年建都史的北京，便是这样一座掩映在遥远笙歌中的戏剧之都。

金　太平多暇　干戈倒载闲兵甲

一一五至一二三四

在北京860余年的建都史上，金朝虽然是开山的朝代，和后面的元、明、清相比却最短。最早"觊觎"燕都之地的金废帝海陵王完颜亮挥师北京，建立金中都，大兴土木将这里打造出盛世国都的风范，同时，作为女真人的代表，他和他的子民一样对汉文化有着如饥似渴的嗜好。事实上不仅海陵王这一代，此后金朝的世代皇族都将汉文化作为代表先进生产力的先进文化进行深入研究和学习，他们学汉字、读汉书、着汉服，将汉族的社会管理方式和教育方式进行积极推广和使用。金朝的很多皇帝都是在文学史上极有地位的诗人，当然，他们写的是汉诗。

金灭亡后，有一些故朝遗老，感叹"金以儒亡"。今人很容易理解成是女真贵族们被强大的汉文化也包括当时汉人引领的社会风尚搞得目眩神迷，纷纷投入和沉醉其中，于是，国之不国。此一说非正史正解，但在某种程度上也表明了那个朝代汉文化的强悍影响力。

电影《霸王别姬》中喜连成科班的班主举着鸡毛掸子教训小学徒好好学戏，说了一句直白托大的话："是人，他就得听戏！"将这句话挪用到金朝的金章宗在位时期，并不夸张。那时节正值金院本朝着杂剧的方向蓬勃发展，当时中国出现了一位对后世戏剧发展有着不可磨灭的深远影响的戏剧家董解元，他的代表作是《西厢记》。

《西厢记》从诞生起至今，究竟有多少剧种、经历了多少次

改编附会、覆盖了多少人次的观众、合计有多少艺人扮演……这些数据一旦有统计必定洋洋大观令人咋舌。2012年，代表北京昆曲最高水平的北方昆曲剧院携这部戏登上了美国肯尼迪艺术中心的舞台；同年底，号称"昆曲义工"的作家白先勇又推出了颇具时尚特色的厅堂版……《西厢记》新闻不断，亮相频频，然而，这些都已经是后来者。当代人最熟悉的《西厢记》实际是"王西厢"，即元代戏剧家王实甫版，而比他更早、因描写爱情和批判封建男权而更具有划时代精神意义且具备了完整戏剧结构最接近现代戏剧创作的《西厢记》，恰是来自金朝的"董西厢"。

董解元的生平资料甚少，有人解释其名字中的解元二字为当时对读书人的尊称。诸多史料中有一点可谓共识，即此人狂放不羁、才华横溢，有极强的驾驭文字和结构故事的能力。"董西厢"的全称是《西厢记诸宫调》，是今存宋金诸宫调中最完整的作品，它标志着那个时代民间文艺的最高水平。

董解元所处的时代，恰逢太平盛世，民间有诸多勾栏、瓦舍集结各种艺人，颇似今天的演艺场所，说故事、杂耍供人观

董解元（生卒年月不详），金戏曲作家，约为金章宗（完颜璟）时人。"解元"两字疑为当时读书人之通称。他根据唐元稹的《莺莺传》创作长篇讲唱文学《西厢记诸宫调》，为元杂剧《西厢记》所本，世称"董西厢"。

赏娱乐。彼时院本盛行，以往流传民间的边讲故事边辅以插科、杂耍的滑稽"戏"正向将演唱、说白相结合的正统"戏曲"演变，院本的演出不仅有了按照故事情节分场次上下连场的演出方式，也有了比较完整的角色、行当。盛行的院本大多描写历史和爱情，特别是表现下层百姓的困苦，嘲讽当权者和针砭时政，但作品大都失传。明朝陶宗仪的《辍耕录》中记载，后世留存的院本名目大约七百多种。清朝张岱在《陶庵梦忆·阮圆海戏》中对金院本有简单记录："其所打院本，又皆主人自制，笔笔勾勒，苦心尽出。"

张岱的话其实适用于董解元制西厢。在今天看来，"董西厢"仍可谓结构宏伟。除说词之外，它共用了包括14种宫调的193套组曲。在这种蝉联而下的组曲中对结构和情节作了苦心经营。其间的起承转合都颇具匠心，情节波澜起伏，引人入胜。尤为有价值的是，"董西厢"有说有唱，曲多白少，语言优美。其创作植根于民间文艺，把诗词中富有表现力的词汇和民间口语熔为一炉，形成朴实浑成的风格。至今，"董西厢"传诵之曲极多。

以"董西厢"为代表的金朝戏剧，直接导致了后世元朝杂剧的鼎盛，同时也成就了下一位"站在前人肩上"继续书写张生和崔莺莺爱情故事的戏剧家王实甫推出他的传世之作《西厢记》。

章节·肆　笙歌 踏戏而行

元 瓦舍勾栏 怒说千古兴亡事
一二七一至一三六八

章节·肆 笙歌 踏戏而行

元朝对北京最大的贡献是留下了一座黄金之城元大都，但遗憾的是，这座举世闻名的繁华都城除了目前可见的静默于北京北土城附近的元大都遗址公园之外，可以寻觅其踪迹的城市遗存少之又少。建筑之不存，或许是当年一代天骄从兴盛到灭亡的宿命表征，后来者空留感喟，仅能凭借史料和类似《马可·波罗行纪》这样的外国人的著述窥见一斑，而吊诡的是，即使这样名满天下的著作，在其究竟是作者的亲历还是作者的编造之间仍争议不休。幸运的是，"大元乾元"的没落终究还是留下了堪与元大都媲美的文化遗产，那就是元杂剧，或者笼统地称之为元曲。

元曲盛行于元代。原本来自所谓的"蕃曲""胡乐",发源于民间,一度指称"街市小令"或"村坊小调"。大都是元曲大家聚集的中心。这些当时的著名作家中有人专制戏剧,有人热衷词曲,因此,元曲天然地包含了元杂剧和散曲这两种为当时的民众所喜闻乐见的艺术形式,于是,也有学者干脆将元曲解释为元代戏曲。无论学界如何争议于象牙塔,有一个共识无可争辩,那就是在中国的元代,在大都这个政治经济文化艺术中心,戏曲的发展达到了鼎盛。

元杂剧的兴盛是站在金院本的肩头完成的。在金院本和诸宫调的直接影响下,元杂剧融合了各种表演艺术形式,并在唐宋以来话本、词曲、讲唱文学的基础上创造了成熟的文学剧本。在元朝,在元大都,无论声名显赫的作家,还是至今已无姓名可考却有作品流传的剧作者,他们苦心经营的杂剧,皆是人民生活的真实反应,并因此为当时的民众所欢迎。

现在对流传下来的元杂剧作品的统计说法互异,通常认为,至今,已发现并保存的、姓名可考的元代作家作品有500种,元代无名氏作品有50种,元明之际无名氏作品187种,合计737种。其中名声最响亮的则是号称元曲四大家的"马关郑白",即马致远、关汉卿、郑光祖和白朴。

在今天的京西门头沟区王平镇的韭园村西落坡小山村内,有一元代古宅,村民们世代相传说这里就是马致远故居。韭园村是"王平古道"的道口,属于北京著名景观京西大道的一支。马致远故居是一座大四合院。门前小桥流水,院内青草丛生,恰恰符合他的代表作《天净沙·秋思》所写的"枯藤老树昏鸦,小桥流水人家,古道西风瘦马,夕阳西下,断肠人在天涯"。

尽管对马致远的生平说法不一，但北京人还是很自豪地认定他是大都人。今人所知马致远一生作杂剧15种，讲昭君出塞故事的杂剧《汉宫秋》是其代表作；散曲120多首，有辑本《东篱乐府》。和大多怀有济世之心的旧文人一样，马致远青年时仕途坎坷，中年才中进士，一生最高的官职是在大都任工部主事，晚年不满时政，隐居田园，以衔杯击缶自娱自乐。作为壮怀激烈的文化人，马致远身后能颇感欣慰的应该是他的文学戏剧成就，他有"曲状元"之称，元末明初贾仲明在诗中说："万花丛中马神仙，百世集中说致远"，"姓名香贯满梨园"，可见其地位。

元曲四大家中还有一位与北京渊源颇深，他是四人中在世界范围内造成深远艺术影响的佼佼者，是中国戏剧发展史上的明星"编剧"，即元朝伟大的戏曲家关汉卿，后世称其为"曲圣"。据文献记载，关汉卿编有杂剧67部，现存18部。个别作品是否出自关汉卿手笔，学术界尚有分歧。其中《窦娥冤》《救风尘》《望江亭》《拜月亭》《鲁斋郎》《单刀会》《调风月》等，是他的代表作。这些剧作流传至今，仍在以不同的样式上演。1958年，他被世界和平大会理事会定为世界文化名人，在中外展开了关汉卿创作700周年纪念活动。同年6月28日晚，国内1500个职业剧团以至少100种不同的戏剧形式同时上演关汉卿的剧本。他的剧作被译为英文、法文、德文、日文等，在世界各地广泛传播，外国人称他为"东方的莎士比亚"。

就像提到莎士比亚的名字便会想到《哈姆雷特》，提到关汉卿则不能不说他一生最杰出的作品《窦娥冤》。年幼家关汉卿（约 1220—1300 年），元代杂剧作家，中国古代戏曲创作的代表人物，"元曲四大家"之首。号已斋（一作一斋）、已斋叟。汉族，解州（今山西省运城）人，与马致远、郑光祖、白朴并称为"元曲四大家"。以杂剧的成就最大，一生写了60 多种，今存 18 种，最著名的有《窦娥冤》。关汉卿也写了不少历史剧，如《单刀会》《单鞭夺槊》《西蜀梦》等。散曲今在小令 40 多首，套数 10 多首。关汉卿塑造的"我却是蒸不烂、煮不熟、捶不匾、炒不爆、响当当一粒铜豌豆"（《不伏老》）的形象也广为人称，被誉"曲家圣人"。

贫的窦娥被转卖又被冤屈处死，其冤情感天动地使六月飞雪，关汉卿将这个悲情故事写得曲折婉转又充满愤懑深刻。窦娥幻想破灭时的愤怒呼喊在今天看来仍为戏剧史上的绝句："为善的受贫穷更命短，造恶的享富贵又寿延。天地也做得个怕硬欺软，却原来也这般顺水推船。地也，你不分好歹何为地！天也，你错勘贤愚枉做天！"窦娥的责天问地，代表着普通人不屈从于现实命运的浩然正气。元杂剧大多充溢着郁闷、愤懑的情绪，这是在异族统治下的元代作家目睹种种社会现象后的自然流露。但关汉卿在《窦娥冤》中表达的是对当时整个社会的否定与诅咒般的诘难，极具震撼力。

拜元代这些伟大的"戏剧工作者"所赐，元杂剧使中国戏剧艺术走向成熟。元杂剧确立了此后绵延百余年的中国戏剧四折一楔子的结构形式，其"一人主唱"与说白相连、"曲白相生"的表演为后世各个剧种所广泛借鉴，而其剧本对舞台性的注重，角色分工的精细和类型化，以及作家流逸的情思与本质性的真实生活相结合等鲜明的个性特征，对后人的戏剧创作产生了深远的影响。

明 民间传奇 花花草草由人恋

一三六八至一六四四

随着元顺帝离开大都再度回到他祖先征战的起点蒙古草原，北京又开始了一个以汉文化为中心的汉人治下的王朝。彼时在元朝已经达到极高水准的杂剧，尤其是元曲四大家的作品，仍在北京民间演出场所勾栏瓦舍中上演。世事多变，但人民群众的文化娱乐生活仍多姿多彩，有时因盛世升平，有时为苦中作乐。

分辨明朝的戏曲发展，可以分为两段：一段是从洪武建国到正德、嘉靖以前，这一时期杂剧从鼎盛走向衰落；嘉靖以后为一个阶段，此时传奇戏空前发展。

明初的杂剧继承了元代杂剧的基本形式而且同元代杂剧一样立足"草根"，伴随着明初社会经济的恢复和发展重新成为民间文化生活中的一项主要内容。但是，大约到永乐中期，杂剧的演出引起了朝廷的重视。永乐九年（1411年）明王朝在北京正式公布了关于杂剧的禁令。这种官方干预决定了杂剧的发展方向必须在当时政治允许的范围之中进行。这项规定可谓"严苛"。例如凡乐人搬作杂剧戏文不许妆扮历代帝王、后妃、忠臣、节烈、先圣、先贤、神象，违者杖一百，官民之家容扮者与同罪。而其神仙、道扮及义夫、节妇、孝子、贤孙、劝人为善者不在禁限。由于如此限制，明初的杂剧几乎只能是以正统的忠孝节义的教化戏、正统的历史戏以及空洞无物的神仙戏为主，与元代杂剧那种大胆揭露社会黑暗、表露人民心声的民众精神完全背道而驰。至此，杂剧不再是民众观照现实、表达心愿和宣泄情绪的载体，也不再受到人们的喜爱，其没落实为必然。

命运关闭一扇门的同时总会顺手打开一扇窗。杂剧没落沦为统治者教化民众的工具，郁闷的文化人找到了更好的表达方式——明传奇戏应运而生。嘉靖之后，北京成了传奇戏发展的中心，南方的大量优秀传奇戏也在这里上演。

明传奇戏在形式上比元杂剧更完备。一个剧本，常有30出左右，分为上、下两部分，结构紧凑，科诨穿插。其音乐采取曲牌联套的形式，一折戏中包含多个宫调，曲牌多少取决于剧情需要，所有登场的角色都可以演唱。明传奇戏包括众多的地方声腔。其中流传最广、影响最深远的是昆山腔和弋阳腔。其中昆山腔经过嘉靖时期魏良辅的改革，创立了委婉细腻、流利悠远的"水磨调"，讲究字清、板正、腔纯，将弦索、箫管、鼓板三类乐器合在一起，建立了规模完整的乐队伴奏。曾经，一出《浣纱记》的演出，使昆山腔通过舞台的光大流布，成为全国性剧种，这便是如今已成为世界级非物质

文化遗产的中国昆曲的雏声。

明朝嘉靖之后的中国，是传奇戏的天下。万历年间，传奇戏创作进入高潮，形式也更丰富，汤显祖是这一时期最重要的剧作家。他的传世之作有《紫钗记》《牡丹亭》《邯郸记》和《南柯记》，世称"玉茗堂四梦"，其中以《牡丹亭》成就最高。事实上用今天的眼光来看，这并非一个悲情故事，而是充满了爱情的欢乐和年轻人对现实生活的享受。《牡丹亭》写名叫杜丽娘的女孩因情而死，又因情复生。其文辞之华美优雅无出其右。在《牡丹亭》之前，中国最具影响的爱情题材戏剧作品是《西厢记》，而《牡丹亭》一问世，便令《西厢记》减色不少。《顾曲杂言》中有如此评说："牡丹亭梦一出，家传户诵，几令西厢减价。"

"花花草草由人恋，生生死死随人愿，便酸酸楚楚无人怨"，《牡丹亭》中的杜丽娘吟唱着这段著名的唱词一直走到今天。1986年，中国南京电影制片厂拍摄了电影版《牡丹亭》，此后，越剧电视连续剧，电视连续剧，芭蕾舞剧，小剧场青春话剧，作家白先勇亲手打造的青春版、北京皇家粮仓的"当家"戏厅堂版以及北方昆曲剧院倾心搬演并在海外巡演的全版昆剧和目前尚未公映的内地与香港合作拍摄的故事片版……多少年来，无论在王谢堂前还是寻常巷里，《牡丹亭》一路喧闹着深受追捧，无论何种形式总能常演不衰。

明传奇戏的繁荣一直延续到清朝，而传奇戏在民间甚至宫廷的深受喜爱和其在声腔、表演方面积累下的经验与逐渐形成的套路，直接影响了清末京剧的诞生和发展。

清 徽汉合流 京腔京韵自多情
一六一六至一九一二

历史上的每个王朝都以其独特的样式将音舞诗画写在苍茫岁月的边边角角，其间有一些文人墨客、戏剧大家，谈笑歌哭皆成粉墨，他们流传下来的有关戏如人生、人生如戏的只言片语抑或鸿篇巨制，作为一个个时代的注解，与史实相辅相成。

中国戏剧一路走到明朝灭亡、清朝立国，仍然沿袭着传奇戏的旧制，彼时昆曲声势已成，但因其主唱南音而难以独霸京师。拥有一国之都地位的北京，正在等待一种能成为国剧的艺术。

时间的指针指向1790年，北京演艺界的主旋律是为80岁的乾隆皇帝祝寿。史料记载当时的演出规模极其盛大，自西华门到西直门外高梁桥沿途十几里路，每隔几十步设一座戏台。南腔北调，四方之乐，令人目不暇接。安庆艺人高朗亭领衔的三庆徽班便是其中活跃的一支。徽班唱徽调，徽调唱的二簧调是西皮和二簧两种曲调的合称，也是后来形成的京剧唱腔的主旋律。将徽调结合汉调以及京师曲韵，形成令北京人耳目一新的新剧，是当时来自安徽、湖北的戏班艺人们最大的贡献，这一年，可以看作中国国粹京剧的发源。

和前朝的戏剧一样，京剧发端于民间，但其发展则有所不同。前朝戏剧成熟于勾栏瓦舍甚至青楼行院，京剧的成熟却阳春白雪到拜皇家推动所赐得以蔚然成气候。

清朝的皇宫贵胄多是戏迷，史上名声响亮的许多制戏圣手来自清末皇族。清代档案记载，最迟到康熙朝时已有管理

咸丰（1831-1861年）对京剧的爱好达到了痴迷的程度，并将戏曲演出列入朝廷仪典定制。咸丰十年（1860年）之后，随商旅往来及戏班的流动演出，京剧很快传播到全国各地。

内廷演戏的机构——南府和景山。乾隆时期，清宫演戏机构庞大，几乎相当于现今十余个国家级演出团体的编制。道光七年改南府为"升平署"。当时内廷演戏的演员即"内廷供奉"多为杰出的民间艺人，如京剧大师谭鑫培、王瑶卿、杨小楼等。

咸丰皇帝是允许京剧进宫演出并对其做出积极评价的第一位清朝皇帝。他经常点戏、看戏，有时还指导太监演戏。他在热河逃难时醉心戏剧。而慈禧则是出名的戏迷，每日必观。2013年4月25日，北京颐和园德和园经历长达18个月的精细修缮之后重新开园，这座修建于晚清的皇家戏园，一度专供"老佛爷"慈禧听戏，仅其中的三层大戏楼即耗银71万两。德和园是京剧艺术走进宫廷的标志，也是宫廷审美品位流向民间的通道——民间艺人进宫演戏，受到宫廷影响又提高了民间演出的旨趣。

对于京剧的发展，慈禧功不可没。史料记载，她听戏时手拿演出剧本，一边欣赏艺人表演，一边检验对错，发现表演有误立刻追究。她给艺人挑毛病总是挑得精准，让艺人不得不服。慈禧还亲自主持剧本改编。归政光绪后她长住颐和园，叫人将《昭代箫韶》翻改成京剧。《昭代箫韶》是杨家将故事，原本240出，其中大部分是昆曲，改编难度颇大。慈禧让身边所有粗通文墨者都来动手，她自己也编了不少唱词。词编出之后让艺人安腔。在戏曲界号称"通天教主"的王瑶卿曾回忆，他善于编创新腔的本事，就是在慈禧太后的逼迫下练出来的。2013年5月7日至16日，慈禧的"文化创意成果"《昭代箫韶》经过改编和整理复排后登陆北京长安大戏院进行为期10天的演出，这是第一部根据清宫连台本戏改造的正宗皇家京剧，此后，北京京剧院和颐和园合作将其打造成德和园的经典驻场演出。

明朝宫廷的禁令使杂剧衰亡，清朝宫廷的重视和推动，则促成了京剧的成熟与壮大。此后，北京出现了各式各样的戏班、专门培养人才的京剧科班以及一代代传承、发展这门戏剧艺术的大师，他们前赴后继。至2010年11月16日，中国京剧被联合国教科文组织保护非物质文化遗产政府间委员会的24个成员国一致通过，正式入选"人类非物质文化遗产代表作名录"，成为北京乃至中国的文化精粹符号之一。

自金代建都至今860余年来，北京时时刻刻影响着中国戏剧的品质，近千年的北京戏剧演出同时也造就了北京的文化。无论金院本、元杂剧、明传奇还是昆曲、京剧，都是从北京出发演变成为波及全国的大剧种。北京历代士大夫及知识分子对戏剧的审美过滤，提高了各剧种的审美品质，使北京的戏剧作品具有恢弘的气魄、深沉的思想内涵以及精美的艺术形式。北京是名副其实的戏剧之都。

章节·肆　笙歌 踏戏而行

71

章节·伍

丹青 炫墨而舞

这些年，很多人说到欧洲的现代派艺术便会提起他的名字。2012年的苏富比春拍上，他的名画《阅读的妇女》以2130万美元被中国买家买走。曾经，他在1944年成为法国共产党中的一员，1945年，中国延安《解放日报》刊发了这一消息。就是这位崇尚自由、个性十足的艺术家毕加索，在1956年7月29日中午11点30分，将别墅大门为中国画家张大千敞开。那天，张大千看到他研习中国画的作品，正惊讶于源远流长的中国画艺的影响之广大，这时，毕加索说："这个世界上谈到艺术，首先是你们中国人有艺术……所以我最莫名其妙的事，就是何以有那么多的中国人、东方人要到巴黎来学艺术？"在后人书写的张大千传记中，谈到他对这件事的理解。最初他隐约以为毕加索出于谦虚和对中国艺术家的客气而如此"溢美"，但当他认真看完艺术家每一幅中国风的"习作"，他开始明白，毕加索是真心被全世界绝无仅有的中国丹青所吸引。

沿着毕加索的赞美回望历史，在中国元朝最兴盛时期，最繁华的黄金都城大都，也有一名叫作马可·波罗的意大利青年发出过感慨，赞叹中国画家在绢帛之上的纵横飞扬仿佛炫墨而舞。

2012年，画家李可染的山水画《万山红遍》以超过2.9325亿元的价格成交，堪称中国画拍卖价之最。然而，细数一代代中国画家的来时道路，追溯他们画艺的师承渊源，便会回到中国本土的丹青技艺上来。北京，这座有860余年建都史的古老城市，在她的烟云过往中，有数不清的一代代丹青圣手，为中国、为这座辉煌的都城，书写了一部与众不同的历史。

金　画千般美景　终不过面向汉文化一番膜拜

一一一五至一二三四

唐太宗李世民的陵墓前有6匹举世闻名的骏马，依次名为飒露紫、拳毛䯄、白蹄乌、特勒骠、青骓、什伐赤，号称昭陵六骏。这6匹马是李世民不同时期转战沙场时的坐骑，都是立过战功的名马，深受他喜爱。今天，如果有空去故宫，便可以看到金人赵霖的传世名作《昭陵六骏图》。原本昭陵六骏以浅浮雕技法雕刻，赵霖以其为蓝本进行创作，马匹造型、动势则有厚石刻风采。这幅画是金代人马画难得的艺术精品。1959年中华人民共和国文化部文物局将其拨故宫博物院收藏。事实上，至今并没有关于画家生平的确切史料，唯有从卷尾金人赵秉文的题跋得知，画家赵霖大约是洛阳人，金世宗完颜雍时期以擅画待诏内廷，而《昭陵六骏图》为其存世孤本。

金代的绘画是少数民族艺术与汉文化融合的产物。这个历经跋涉到达北京的少数民族王朝，根基里的彪悍随着王国的日渐稳定而渐渐收敛，取而代之的是虽短暂却也歌舞升平的小盛世。金王朝重视书画，在秘书监下设有书画局，将从宋内府劫掠的书画悉数存入书画局，供贵族和宫廷画家研习，因此金代绘画深受宋画影响。然而，终究是马上的民族，其精神"家底"决定了总不能规避的那些体现着深刻民族性的题材，无论骏马如风、塞外苦寒、激流峭壁……画风是汉人的画风，内里还是白山黑水滋养的情怀。

在吉林省博物馆藏的金人张某的《文姬归汉图卷》是金代

绘画艺术的精品。至今，关于名字已经不存的这位张姓画家只能大致推断出其生活的时代是金章宗时期。《文姬归汉图卷》描绘的是汉末才女蔡文姬一行人归汉途中，冒着漠北大风艰难行进的场景。美术史对这幅作品给予了高度评价："人物众多而主次分明，神情生动而描绘精到，虽未描绘环境，但通过人物畏寒的刻画，突现了路途遥遥和荒塞风沙之苦。画法的精工，极近宋人。"此外，在台北故宫博物院，有金人武元直的纸本水墨《赤壁图》。曾经，对于此画是否金人画作尚有过不小的争议。这幅画颇得宋画的神韵，即使展现惊涛拍岸的流湍之势，也已经完全是文人雅致、汉家风骨。

金代画作留存甚少，杨仁恺在《国宝沉浮录》一书中说："可明确认定为金人作品者不及十件，有几件已流往国外。"北京作为金代的都城62年，只有如此稀少的艺术品流传于世，不能不说是极大的遗憾。蒙古军攻打金中都时，金帝完颜亮以岐国公主、童男童女各500名、彩绣衣3000件和御马3000匹以及金银珠宝等向成吉思汗求和，蒙古军退兵，但金中都已成孤城。1214年，金迁都河南开封定名为南京，随后，蒙古骑兵烧毁了这座曾经被海陵王完颜亮"精雕细琢"以为他的子孙可以千秋万代一统江山的豪华都城。正如当年项羽烧毁了阿房宫，没人知道其中有多少珍宝"殉国"，至今，面对"不及十件"的金代绘画遗产，是否可以猜想当年蒙古军队的那一把火，或许也将许多珍贵的艺术品烧得荡然无存？

元 画四时佳期 不外穷毕生功力开一代先河

一二七一至一三六八

当蒙古军以摧枯拉朽之势灭掉金朝之后，北京迎来了历史上无限荣耀的一段辉煌至奢华的时光。故纸堆中的史料通常板着面孔，遣词造句务求严谨，而写到元大都，各方史料却不约而同地华丽起来，不惜堆砌起精美的辞藻以描述这座引来全世界瞩目的"黄金之城"。也许元大都太美，于是必须遭遇毁灭——若不如此，回忆和向往还有什么诱人之处呢？

繁华盛世滋养高逸的士大夫和散逸的文化人，元大都便是这样一处丹青乐土。元代立国之初，艺术家特别是汉人艺术家，无论生活和创作，都有滋有味、极尽自由。出身游牧民族的蒙古族统治者在教育程度、文化艺术素养等方面，与中原士大夫之间存在较大的差距，要巩固统治，则需要重视汉文化，从儒家经典中学习治国之道。元世祖忽必烈广收"遗逸"，重用汉族儒臣，到了元仁宗和元文宗时期，更加礼遇文士，尤其喜好书画艺术。元文宗甚至一度建立奎章阁，任命画家、书画鉴藏家柯九思为鉴书博士，对内府所藏书画进行鉴别查定，元朝的翰墨之盛以文宗时为最。

开放的社会带来艺术家个性的展示与发展，元代的绘画发展完全是波澜径自流似的无拘无束，也正因此，迎合了文人情怀，使文人画成为画坛主流。元代没有专门的画院，除少

赵孟頫（1254－1322年），字子昂，号松雪、松雪道人，又号水精宫道人、鸥波，中年曾作孟俯，汉族，吴兴（今浙江湖州）人，元代著名画家，楷书四大家（欧阳询、颜真卿、柳公权、赵孟頫）之一。赵孟頫博学多才，能诗善文，懂经济，工书法，精绘艺，擅金石，通律吕，解鉴赏。特别是书法和绘画成就最高，开创元代新画风，被称为"元人冠冕"。他也善篆、隶、真、行、草书，尤以楷、行书著称于世。

数专业画家直接服务于宫廷外，大都是身居高位的士大夫画家和在野的文人画家。他们热衷表现自身的生活环境、情趣和理想。山水、枯木、竹石、梅兰等题材大量出现，与金朝相比，直接反映社会生活的人物画减少，作品更加强调文学性和笔墨韵味，重视以书法用笔入画和诗、书、画的结合。在中国绘画史上，元代被认为是中国文人画继承古代意蕴同时开一代先河的时期，元代绘画对后世绘画的发展与创新产生的影响可谓空前。

元大都作为全国绘画中心的地位直到元末才发生变化，因统治式微，绘画中心转移到江南。元代前期的大都绘画非常繁荣，著名的宫廷画家有何澄、刘贯道、李肖岩、刘元等，他们擅长肖像画、人物画、宗教画和界画，延续着早已吸收了宋代经验的金代传统。而真正为元朝绘画开创新风的画家，则是宋宗室后裔赵孟頫。

赵孟頫是宋太祖赵匡胤的第11世孙、秦王赵德芳的嫡派子孙,字子昂,号松雪。他的父亲曾任宋朝户部侍郎兼知临安府浙西安抚使,宋朝灭亡后,归故乡闲居。然而,正如今天所说,是金子在哪里都闪光。"能诗善文、懂经济、工书法、精绘艺、擅金石、通律吕、解鉴赏"的赵孟頫仍然被急需修《世祖实录》的元成宗召回大都,即便他借病乞归,仍紧抓不放;此后,无论皇帝还是皇太子都对他颇有"兴趣";最终,他于延祐三年(1316年)官居一品,名满天下,同时也因"仕元""失节"而遭诟病,直至后世被讲究气节的文人墨客"薄其人遂薄其书",留下无穷争议。

尽管经历了矛盾复杂、荣华尴尬的一生,但是,没人能否认赵孟頫作为一代书画大家的地位。他一生取得的书法和绘画成就被称为"元人冠冕",后人评价其作品"先画后书此一纸,咫尺之间兼二美",事实上他的书画诗印四绝,在他在世时已名传中外。史料记载元大都盛况中亦曾提及,当年日本、印度人士以珍藏赵孟頫的作品为贵,他可算是历史上为北京的中外文化交流作出贡献的先驱。

作为一位变革转型时期承前启后的大家,赵孟頫提出"作画贵有古意"的口号,扭转了北宋以来古风渐湮的画坛颓势,

使绘画从工艳琐细之风转向质朴自然；他提出以"云山为师"的口号，强调画家的写实基本功与实践技巧，克服"墨戏"的陋习；他提出"书画本来同"的口号，以书法入画，使绘画的文人气质更为浓烈；他提出"不假丹青笔，何以写远愁"的口号，以画寄意，使绘画的内在功能得到深化，涵盖更为广泛……在元大都层出不穷的优秀艺术家之中，赵孟頫是一位在人物、山水、花鸟、马兽诸画科皆有成就，画艺全面并有创新的全才。中国绘画史对他的评价极高，认为他在南北一统、蒙古族入主中原的政治形势下，吸收南北绘画之长，复兴中原传统画艺，维持并延续了其发展，与诸多少数民族美术家共同繁荣中华文化，开创了元代文人画新画风，并以此影响后世，为文人画在日后登堂入室进入主流拉开了序幕。

在赵孟頫和与他"携手"进行艺术实践的大都艺术家的深远影响下，伴随着元朝统治的风雨飘摇，推动中国画坛发展的任务落在了接过赵氏衣钵的江南画家们肩上。无论以《富春山居图》著称的黄公望还是与他并称"元四家"的王蒙、吴镇和倪瓒，他们形成的鲜明时代风貌，有力地推动了后世绘画艺术的蓬勃发展。

画京畿胜景 袭古人启变法成繁荣之风

明 一三六八至一六四四

章节·伍 丹青 炫墨而舞

明朝的开国皇帝朱元璋和他之后的明成祖朱棣都是中国文人画的拥趸，虽然他们以武起家、凭武定国，但这并不妨碍他们重视中国传统艺术的保护和发展。明朝是在金元两个少数民族政权之后的汉人政权，在朱明王朝的大多数王公贵胄、文人雅士看来，以汉儒文化为根基的中国画迎来了可以担当承前启后历史重任的绝好机会。

中国历史上的每一个朝代都是从国定而泰初发展到繁荣盛世再到不得不唱着一曲走向历史深处的哀歌渐渐退出历史舞台。明朝也如出一辙。因此，明朝的绘画演变和发展也是亦步亦趋地附和着这条脉络，一路起承转合。

明朝虽然没有像宋朝那样专门设立画院，但却像南宋一样以灵活的方式任用宫廷画家。随着宫廷绘画兴盛，北京成为全国的绘画中心，其中外地来京画家成为最主要的力量，也带来了融合全国各家画派特色的全新创作风。

明代前期，北京的一些擅长山水墨竹的文人画家，以善书供职明廷，作画兼有文人画家和宫廷画家的双重特点。提到这一时期的北京宫廷画，不能不提的便是当时的著名画家王绂和他的代表作《北京八景图》。王绂是由元入明的文人书画家，永乐元年（1403年）以善书被荐举，供事文渊阁，官至中书舍人，直至去世。《北京八景图》是他扈从皇帝在永乐十一年（1413年）、十二年（1414

年）巡守北京所作，现存中国国家博物馆。可以说这是目前有史料记载的最早关于北京风光的山水图卷，也是历史上描绘北京风光的重要作品。图卷以水墨画北京八景，即金台夕照、太液清波、琼岛春阴、玉泉垂虹、居庸叠翠、蓟门烟树、卢沟晓月和西山霁雪。美术史记载："卷中八景，气象各异。近山短披麻皴，松秀华滋，苔点繁密，状似碎石，沉着有力；远山一抹，平涂擦染，高旷空灵。凡屋舍、桥亭、人物、云烟、流水、无不精致，别有神韵，尚有宋、元山水画遗意。图卷虽无名款，但却是王绂绘画的风格。"王绂以墨竹闻名天下，"笔致纵横洒落，能于运劲中见姿媚，山水风格苍盛"，他一度被赞誉为当时的"国朝第一手"，代表着北京作为全国艺术中心的高端水准。

明代是中国绘画大发展的时期，高手辈出，画风迭变，画派繁兴。在绘画的门类、题材方面，传统的人物画、山水画、花鸟画盛行，文人墨戏画的梅、兰、竹及杂画等也相当发达。以北京为中心的艺术繁盛也带动了民间绘画和壁画的发展。

明朝绘画中涌现出强调勾勒设色的重彩人物画，至今，仍有同类手法和风格的壁画留存，北京法海寺壁画便是其佼佼者。法海寺位于北京西郊的翠微山南麓，为明代正统间太监李童集资所建。其大雄宝殿内的《帝释梵天图》，由工部营缮所画士

官宛福清、王恕，画士张平、王义、顾行、李原、潘福、徐福林等人绘制，描绘以帝释、梵天为中心的诸天，构图繁复而多变化，刻画突出了性格神情，画法则继承唐宋遗法，浓彩重施，沥粉贴金，风格精密繁丽，反映了宫廷绘画对唐宋佛教壁画传统的承继。

开明的政治环境和平稳的社会、经济发展，往往会带来艺术上的创新和求变。对于明朝后期的中国画坛，最重要的历史性大事，是"西风东渐"。

讲到这里，绕不开的名字是利玛窦和汤若望，这两位来自欧洲的传教士为中国绘画带来了最初的西洋风。他们一先一后不约而同地以向当朝皇帝进献西洋圣像的方式，让中国人见识了西洋绘画。万历二十八年即1600年，意大利天主教耶稣会传教士利玛窦（Matteo Ricci，1552—1610年）入京晋见万历皇帝，

利玛窦(1552-1610年),意大利耶稣会传教士,学者。明朝万历年间来到中国居住。其原名中文直译为玛提欧·利奇,利玛窦是他的中文名字,号西泰,又号清泰、西江。王应麟所撰《利子碑记》上说:"万历庚辰有泰西儒士利玛窦,号西泰,友辈数人,航海九万里,观光中国。"

汤若望(1592-1666年),字道未,意大利耶稣会传教士,天主教耶稣会修士、神父、学者。在中国生活47年,历经明、清两个朝代,顺治朝封为"光禄大夫",官至一品(一级正品)。逝世后安葬于北京利玛窦墓左侧。在科隆有故居,塑有雕像。在意大利耶稣会档案馆有他大量资料。

所贡方物中有"时画天主圣像一幅,古画天主圣像一幅",取得"留京工作"的资质后又进献西画三幅,分别画的是西班牙皇宫、罗马圣马可教堂和威尼斯广场。这是最初传入中国的西画,其中的圣像供奉于北京宣武门内天主教堂。曾经有观者记载,所供圣母像"其貌如生,身与臂手,俨然隐起帧上,脸之凸凹处正视与生人不殊"。这种具有视觉幻象的西洋画法,引起了明代艺术家的浓厚兴趣,欲知其所以然,对此利玛窦说:"中国画但画阳,不画阴,故看之人面躯正平,无凸凹相。吾国画兼阴与阳写之,故面有高下,而手臂皆轮圆耳。"利玛窦还把西洋雕版画带到中国。在利玛窦之后,日耳曼传教士汤若望也来京进呈《天主耶稣返都像》《耶稣方钉刑架像》和《天主耶稣立架像》。这些天主教圣像通过教堂、墨谱和摹刻本对中国的绘画发生了影响,这种影响一直流布到清朝,渐成风气。

清 画万方智慧 树一国经典蕴后世中兴

一六一六至一九一一

伴随着明清易代,中国历史上最后一个汉家王朝明朝湮没于历史的烟波浩渺之中。但正如女真人建立的金朝和蒙古人建立的元朝一样,清朝的建立并未改变北京作为全国政治文化中心的地位,从清兵入关、顺治登基、定都北京到末代皇帝溥仪逊位,北京始终是主流绘画的中心,同时表现出上承古人、重视传统又兼收并蓄、开放包容的特点。满族的入主中原,更造就了一批宗室画家、满族画家。

清朝的绘画发展,流派纷呈,西风日盛,才人迭出,蔚为壮观。清朝的宫廷绘画与前朝不同,在文人雅趣的基础上,绘画增加了纪实甚至"辅政"的功能。所谓"辅政"可以理解为有组织、有策划、有规模的纪实性创作,颇似"跟踪报道",只是"报道"或"记录"的对象是皇帝和重大政治事件。比如,诞生在康熙盛世的纪实性绘画《康熙南巡图》。康熙皇帝在位期间,为巩固统治,有6次著名的南下视察,后世关于康熙下江南和乾隆在江南的多次微服私访有许多戏说版本流传民间。但《康熙南巡图》为后人留下了康熙皇帝相对真实的行程。据史料记载,在第一次南巡之后,康熙下令征召画家,全程描绘1691年的第二次南巡。为此清廷聘请职业画家王进京为首席宫廷画家,带领诸多宫廷画家一起创作,历时6年,绘成12卷,12卷前后衔接又各自成幅,详尽描绘了康熙第二次南巡活动,以及沿途所经的城镇乡村、山川名胜、风土人情，场面宏大，人物众多，堪称古今纪实绘画的巨制。出身于绘画世家的王翚当时已有"画圣"之称。他以60岁高龄来京主绘南巡图，在北京居留8年，对北京绘画产生了极大影响。如今，《康熙南巡图》已成无价之宝，12卷中只有第1、9、10、11、12卷藏于北京故宫博物院，其他各卷分别藏于美国、法国及加拿大等国的博物馆或私人手中。尽管如此，从在北京故宫可以得见的5卷，仍可看到当时宫廷画师的精湛技艺，也能看出清代纪实性绘画强大的"宣传"功能。

清代的宫廷画家队伍庞大，名满天下者甚众，清代各时期的作品流传至今的颇多。事实上在承担纪实、"辅政"责任的职业画家之外，还有许多"供奉内廷"的画家是"词臣画家"，他们能诗能文亦擅长书法丹青，这些人一面承袭古人衣钵发展传统中国绘画，一面凭借自身的见识广博、得风气之先，将以当时的社会开放程度所决定可以接触到的最新绘画技法和艺术理念应用到中国美术创新中来。能佐证清朝一度以开放的心态在艺术上广采众家之长的重大史实，则是自康熙以来频频在宫廷画家中任用来自西方的传教士画家。

西洋画家为北京画坛带来"西风"起源于明朝晚期，如果说曾经备受礼遇的利玛窦和见证过明清之间江山易主的汤若望只是带着西方绘画作品来"行贿"皇家以传播宗教，那么，及至清代，传教士中颇有些掌握西方绘画技能的美术人才，被清廷吸收为宫廷画家，从康熙末年开始直至乾隆朝持续不断。这些在北京的皇宫中以绘画谋生、谋功名的"洋人画家"中，以郎世宁、艾启蒙、安德义和王致诚最为著名，其中又以郎世宁影响最大、作品留传最多。直至今日，郎世宁的作品只要出现在拍卖场上，总会引起极大关注。2000年，香港佳士得春拍推出他的《萍野鸣秋》，拍出1764.5万港元的高价；在香港佳士得当年秋拍中，他的《秋林群鹿图》又以884.5万港元拍出，可见其画作的市场号召力经久不衰。

1715年，意大利传教士郎世宁远涉重洋来到中国，被重视西洋技艺的康熙皇帝召入宫中，从此开始了长达50多年的宫廷画家生涯。由于郎世宁带来了西洋绘画技法，向皇帝和其他宫廷画家展示了欧洲明暗画法的魅力，他先后受到了康熙帝、雍正帝、乾隆帝的重用。他是一位艺术上的全才，人物、肖像、走兽、花鸟、山水无所不涉、无所不精，成为雍正帝、乾隆帝时宫廷绘画的代表人物。在绘画创作中，郎世宁融中西技法于一体，形成精细逼真的效果，创造出了新的画风，同时，他也深谙中国宫廷的"做人艺术"，他严格遵守作画前绘制稿本、待皇帝批准后再"照样准画"的清宫绘画制度，将创新以温和、隐蔽的方式缓慢推进，不疾不徐地在艺术实践中将欧洲的绘画技法传授给中国宫廷画家，使清代的宫廷绘画带有"中西合璧"的特色，呈现出不同于历代宫廷绘画的新颖画貌和独特风格。

郎世宁在他78周岁生日的前3天，病逝于北京，丧礼备极哀荣，其遗骸安葬在北京城西阜成门外的欧洲传教士墓地内，乾隆亲撰墓志铭，以示怀念。郎世宁在中国度过了51年，他为200多年前中国与欧洲的文化艺术交流作出了重要和积极的贡献。他的艺术创作都以中国的人和事为题材，其生平和艺术已经成为中国美术史的重要组成部分。郎世宁死后被赐予侍郎之衔，在总计536卷的《清史稿》里，对他的全部记述是："郎世宁，西洋人。康熙中入值，高宗（乾隆）尤赏异。凡名马、珍禽、

异草,辄命图之,无不栩栩如生。设色奇丽,非秉贞等所及。"

　　与西洋风日盛相映成辉的是清末民间绘画的繁荣。曾经,中国绘画特别是文人画一度是儒人雅士的专属,在清朝晚期,则以王谢堂前燕飞入寻常百姓家。当然,此"燕"非彼"燕",在北京百姓的生活中代表着情趣与点缀着小幸福因而深受喜爱的灯画、扇子画等,比中规中矩的"雅画"更质朴亲民。灯画是绘制在纱灯绢片上的工笔画;扇子画则顾名思义,即可制成扇子的扇面画。这些民间画的题材以流行小说、戏曲中的人物故事为主,《西游记》《列国志》《今古奇观》等传奇话本无不可以入画。在清朝晚期的北京,琉璃厂、隆福寺等热闹的商业街上,许多画店和笺扇店的生意都非常好,形成了繁荣的民间绘画市场。

　　清代绘画的发展中不容小觑的便是美术理论的发展,其表现在于艺术家、理论家的著录书籍十分丰富,堪称集历代著录书之大成。

　　在北京这片土地上,究竟还有多少曾经在860余年间炫墨而舞的艺术家尚未被发现?还有多少代表着中国绘画发展史上各个时期的风骚、延续着北京艺术之脉的作品还没有被发掘?

　　北京有世界上绝无仅有的皇家宫殿紫禁城,她同时还是中国最大的古代文化艺术博物馆。860余年间的绘画孤品、绝品,这里都有收藏。这里有纸绢类元代书画130多件,有明代包括吴门画派在内的诸多名家精品,有清代宫廷画和西洋画家供奉内廷的传世之作⋯⋯假如想看中国美术史上最辉煌、最繁荣、最具创造力、最有中国特色的经典作品,来北京,足矣。

章节·陆 绮韵 寄世而吟

花貌倾颓事已遣。浩语虚掷竟念矣。江山王气巷七十劫枷。春去秋又一轮，横，鸳峰，撼寒凋。野花平碧残唾中鹃，正之大河限人间世，莽，魚悅归到酒里。

身为中国人，一旦走入茫茫书海，常常能遇见这样的名字：史景迁、孔飞力、马伯乐、葛兰言、费正清、傅高义……许许多多这样用美丽的中国汉字写出的诗意名字，令人不由猜想，他们该是如何的家学渊源。然而，事实上他们并不是中国人，而是一生致力于汉学研究的外国学者。也许是太过热爱中国文化，他们从中国典籍、诗文之中选取了既能与自己的名字谐音又能体现其高标自许的中文名字。他们的名字与他们的作品彼此辉映着，让中国读者备感亲切。

现代人之中，有多少人在捧读中国古典诗词和历代典籍？其数据不可考。但即便是年轻的北京少年，啜饮着东西方融合的文化琼浆，一定不会对这样的电影名字感到陌生——《一树梨花压海棠》《魂断蓝桥》《此情可问天》……这些人们耳熟能详的域外电影经典，曾经分别叫做《洛丽塔》《滑铁卢大桥》《霍华德庄园》……当它们还是原名的时候，中国观众可能完全无法猜想其内容，然而，当它们以美丽的中文名字出现时，中国观众则格外会心，哦，原来，《洛丽塔》是一个"十八新娘八十郎"的故事，《滑铁卢大桥》是一场发生在这座著名大桥上的爱情悲剧，而《霍华德庄园》是在讲尽管"天长地久有时尽"却在其后仍然绵延不绝的美好感情。

中国文化的力量有多么强大？也许，这只是区区两个小例子。中国诗词有多么优美？也许，从这两个小例子只能约略窥见一斑。中国文学特别是诗词发展的历史，是一条奔流不息、珠玑随处可见的浩荡江河。这其中，拥有860余年建都史的北京，掀起了一波波巨浪，巨浪翻涌而过，洒遍京畿的是难以尽数的文化珍宝。

金 生逢艰难时世总是诗人的福气

一一五至一二三四

北京的都城史自金海陵王完颜亮1153年定北京为金中都始。这位以上不得台面的机巧手段和玉面狼心的杀戮获取王位的"京城第一帝",同时还是女真族人中深爱汉文化又深得汉文化精髓的诗文大家。

但凡在历史上有建树的帝王,大多也是很勤勉的读书人。完颜亮的少年时代浸淫于诗文,用今天的话说,写作是他练武和学习兵法之余的一大乐事。史料记载,他做藩王时,曾像汉族文士那样为人题写扇面,挥笔写下"大柄若在手,清风满天下",于不经意中展露了不同凡响的帝王志向。待到他真的得遂凌云之志,真的入主金中都并从1153年开始志在将北京建设得"越来越像一座空前的大国都城",他的笔底也越发波澜起伏、壮怀激烈。曾经,志在开疆拓土的他亲征至维扬(今扬州中北部),眼望江左,诗兴与豪情勃发,当即赋诗一首:"万里车书尽会同,江南岂有别疆封。提兵百万西湖上,立马吴山第一峰。"这种帝王气魄被《大金国志》称赞为"一咏一吟,冠绝当时"。

历来,以诗传世的文人常常不能以词与自身的诗歌成就平分秋色,即便如李白、杜甫这样的圣手,往往也是更工于其中一种,犹如人的左右手各擅其能。但完颜亮是一个例外,他不仅诗写得好,作词也独树一帜。史料载完颜亮"使御前都统骠骑大将军韩夷耶射雕军二万三千围,子细军一万,先下两淮;

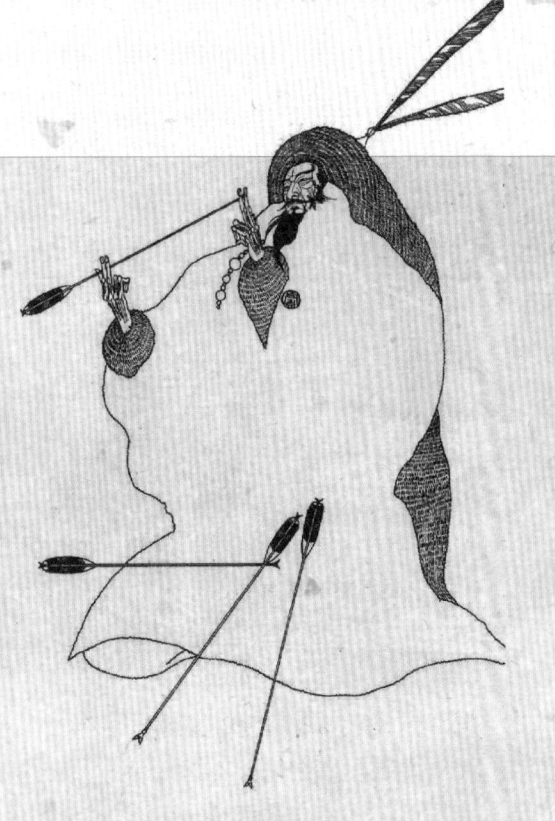

完颜亮（1122-1161年），女真名迪古乃，字元功，金代第四位皇帝。完颜亮为金太祖完颜阿骨打庶长孙，完颜宗干次子，母大氏，史称海陵王。完颜亮在位12年，迁都燕京之后，完善中央集权，进一步巩固了金王朝的统治。在金朝历史上，完颜亮的确是一位颇有作为的皇帝。1161年，完颜亮在南宋境内的瓜洲渡江作战时死于内乱，时年40岁。

临发，赐所制《喜迁莺》以为宠"。这首《喜迁莺·赐大将军韩夷耶》便是一首用典丰富、个性鲜明的豪放词："旌麾初举，正力健，嘶风江渚。射虎将军，落雕都尉，绣帽锦袍翘楚。怒磔戟髯争奋，卷地一声击鼓。笑谈顷，指江南齐楚，六师飞渡。此去无自堕。金印如斗，独在功名取。断锁机谋，垂鞭方略，人事本无今古。试展卧龙韬韫，果见成功旦莫。问江左，想云霓望切，玄黄迎路。"从这首词，也能看出海陵王对中原典故的熟悉，所谓"腹中饱存诗书"。

完颜亮最终没能成就他一生期许的霸业，身后格外凄凉。1161年9月，他在南宋境内的瓜州渡江作战，被浙西兵马都统制完颜元宜等砍伤，而后被用绳勒死，并以大氅裹尸而焚，时年仅40岁。金世宗大定二年（1162年）四月，他被降封为海陵郡王，大定二十一年（1181年）正月，由于早年被他杀害的金熙宗被供入太庙，又再被降为海陵庶人。完颜亮奠基金中都，却最终没能以皇帝的名号将自己写入史册。然而历史很公平，时间的沙并没有抹去他一生中灿烂的诗词成就，相反，为后人留下了这些读来唏嘘的传世名篇。

在海陵王完颜亮之后，金代的诗词首先在帝王之家有了长足的发展，此后以金世宗完颜雍、完颜允恭父子和金章宗为代表的女真诗人的作品，体现了思想观念上的进一步儒学化和审美心理上的中原化。此时的金代诗坛，诗人辈出，作品繁多。与中国历史上的其他朝代相比，金朝历史相对短暂，到了金后期，金朝在蒙古的进逼下国势逐渐衰微，成为干戈缭乱的艰难时世，但这时的诗词创作却相当活跃，产生了一批关心国运和民生的好作品，也产生了元好问这样一位在中国文学史上留下独特光彩的诗、论大家。

元好问（1190—1257年）祖先出于北魏鲜卑拓跋氏，算是真正的"世家子"。他32岁登进士第，曾任南阳等县的县令，后入朝任右司都事、东曹都事等职。金亡之时，他被元兵押解到聊城，然后回到家乡从事著述。元好问是金代最重要的诗人，他存诗1400余首，作品之富在金代诗坛首屈一指。

元好问的一生遭际，充分印证了"国家不幸诗家幸，赋到沧桑句便工"。他亲身经历了亡国惨痛，个人遭遇与民族、国家的命运息息相关，他的"纪乱诗"展示了金、元易代之际的历史风云。他的诗中既有对国家灭亡、人民遭难的现实的哀叹，又有寓悲壮慷慨于苍莽雄阔的意境。在蒙古军围攻汴京城时，他写下了著名的《壬辰十二月车驾东狩后即事五首》之二："惨澹龙蛇日斗争，干戈直欲尽生灵。高原水出山河改，战地风来草木腥。精卫有冤填瀚海，包胥无泪哭秦庭。并州豪杰知谁在，莫拟分军下井陉。"可见其情感悲凉而骨力苍劲的独特诗风。

元好问擅长各种诗体，尤以七律的成就最为突出，他也是金代最杰出的词人，现存词作300余首。

　　元好问对中国文学史的另一大贡献体现在他为了保存金元一代的文献，在金亡之后，编成《中州集》十卷，附《中州乐府》一卷。全书收录金代的251位诗人的2026首诗作，且每人名下各有小传，或叙生平事迹，或评所作诗文，旨在以诗存史。《中州集》具有重要的文献价值，是金代历史的宝贵史料。

元 文理与世推移 江山代有诗词歌赋
一二七一至一三六八

不知多少人念过"一代天骄成吉思汗,只识弯弓射大雕"这样的诗句,惊叹于大汗气魄之余也难免会猜测,热衷征战的马上民族即便执掌天下,又能有多少文采?沿着这个思路,很多人以为元世祖忽必烈不通文墨,却想不到《全元诗》第一首《陟玩春山纪兴》便出自他之手。在写遍"韶景""花色""垆烟""琴声"后,这位将北京缔造成当时为全世界所艳羡与向往的"黄金之都"元大都的一代君王笔锋一转,写下气势恢宏的最后一句:"净刹玉毫瞻礼罢,回程仙驾驭苍龙。"其眼界、胸怀,在当时无人出其右。

就像金朝的皇帝们一样,元朝的每位皇帝都对汉文化充满敬仰并积极学习,这种自皇家波及朝野、文坛、书院及至市井的各民族文化互相学习、彼此融合之风,成就了元朝的文学发展,诞生了与唐诗、宋词并驾的散曲和大量至今脍炙人口的杂剧,同时,也让后人有机会瞻仰许许多多优秀的少数民族诗人、词人的名篇佳作。

从1271年元世祖忽必烈首建大元,到1368年明太祖朱元璋在应天(今南京)称帝建立明朝,其间有两位在今天仍为世人称颂的少数民族诗人分别傲立于近百年时光的两端,前者是被成吉思汗"发掘"并"延请"而后在忽必烈时期达到政治生涯最高点的契丹贵族耶律楚材(1190—1244年),后者是在元后期名满江湖的诗画大家萨都剌（1272—1355年）。

1215年，成吉思汗的蒙古大军攻占燕京，听说耶律楚材满腹经纶、才华横溢，遂向他询问治国大计。而耶律楚材也因对大金失去信心，决心转投成吉思汗帐下以拯救处于水深火热中的百姓。他的到来，对成吉思汗及其子孙产生了深远影响，他采取的各种措施为元朝的建立奠定了基础。

耶律楚材是杰出的政治家，出身于契丹贵族家庭，生长于燕京（今北京），世居金中都（今北京），是辽太祖耶律阿保机的九世孙。耶律楚材除了在政治上极有建树外，在文化艺术方面亦有卓越成就和多种贡献。他是中国第一位提出经度概念的人，编有《西征庚午元历》，还主持修订了《大明历》。他曾随从成吉思汗和窝阔台远征四方，写下大量诗歌，其《湛然居士集》收录了660余首诗。他熟悉边疆的风土人情、山川景物，在诗中描绘了奇瑰壮丽的西域风光。其西域诗有50余首，这些诗篇是后人研究西域历史的重要参考资料。耶律楚材尤其擅写律诗，诗文集中尤多七律，韵律流畅沉稳，风骨雄健豪放。耶律楚材也能填词，如《鹧鸪天·题七真洞》："花界倾颓事已迁，浩歌遥望意茫然。江山王气空千劫，桃李春风又一年。横翠嶂，架寒烟。野花平碧怨啼鹃。

不知何限人间梦，并触沈思到酒边？"词中化用黄庭坚的诗句表达对世事变迁的感慨，可谓字字珠玑。耶律楚材作为契丹后人，十分重视保存辽代文化。现存辽代篇幅最长的契丹语诗篇《醉义歌》就是由他译为汉文七言歌行体长诗并保存于《湛然居士文集》中。

耶律楚材在成吉思汗、窝阔台汗两朝任事近30年，公元1244年的五月十四日去世。消息传出，倾国悲哀。汉族的士大夫更是流泪凭吊这位功勋卓著的契丹族政治家。元世祖中统二年（1261年），忽必烈遵从他的遗愿，将他的遗骸移葬于故乡北京玉泉山以东的瓮山，即今天北京颐和园的万寿山。即使抛开其政治上的贡献，仅就其文化上的贡献而言，耶律楚材也是足以彪炳史册的巨人。

在元朝诗坛与耶律楚材齐名的少数民族艺术家是萨都剌。他同样才华横溢，身兼诗人、画家、书法家。因其先世为西域人，他本人出生于雁门（今山西代县），一度被称为"雁门才子"。萨都剌一生留下将近800首诗词，内容既有对山川风物的描述也有对宫廷生活的记录，更有怀古伤今描写百姓生活和直指社会不平的诗作。他的诗集名为《雁门集》，至今流传。《新元史》称赞萨都剌的诗"诗才清丽，冠绝一时"。

萨都剌的与众不同在于他长于思考、对社会人生有独到见解，他在许多诗中表达了自己对人生、对社会的看法。他为人正直，做官清廉，因此对于有操守的同僚，每每赠诗。如《寄朱县尹》一诗："地僻民安业，官清县少衙。江东贤令尹，心地似梅花。"他身处元朝中后期，当时的农民起义此起彼伏，目睹战争惨状，诗人也心急如焚。他在《题画马图中》写道"要

耶律楚材（1190-1244年），契丹族，杰出政治家，蒙古帝国时期大臣。1215年，成吉思汗的蒙古大军攻占燕京时候，听说他才华横溢、满腹经纶，遂向他询问治国大计。而耶律楚材也因对腐朽的大金失去信心，决心转投成吉思汗帐下以拯救处于水深火热中的百姓。他的到来，对成吉思汗及其子孙产生深远影响，他采取的各种措施为元朝的建立奠定了基础。

令四海无战争，千古万古歌太平"，表达了反对战争、热爱和平的愿望。

在萨都剌传世的作品中，可以明显地看到，他深得古人之意，以魏晋和盛唐诗为宗，言之有物，渗透于字里行间的是浓浓的"情"字。元代诗人虞集十分推崇萨都剌的诗，称赞其诗"最长于情，流丽清婉"。与萨都剌同时代的大诗人杨维桢也认为他的诗"风流俊爽，修本朝家范"。当代著名学者章培恒在一篇谈及元代诗歌艺术的文章中认为，在元朝中后期，"元诗迎来了最后的，也是其发展史上成就最高的一个阶段——顾嗣立所谓'奇材益出'的'至正之末'。'奇材'最杰出的代表，则为萨都剌与杨维桢"。可见萨都剌把整个元代诗歌艺术推到了后人须仰视才可顾及的高度。

明 盛世乱世身为重臣者常有写意情怀

一三六八至一六四四

若以中国文学史上的"灿烂"作为分类的依据，随着唐诗、宋词、元曲一路而下至明朝，最卓越的文学创作当是小说。有明一代，诗词的发展并不是最显赫、最辉煌。但中国诗词发展自有其不断传承和创新，即便是在以小说、传奇、话本为热的明朝，仍有许多工于诗词的大家制出广为流传的经典名作。

在近300年的明代历史上，无论诗人或诗作的数量，都超过前代，这一时期中国诗词发展的道路较为曲折。明初洪武、建文年间，大部分诗人模拟唐人趋势"各抒心得"，"隽旨名篇，自在流出"；到了永乐至天顺年间，则出现了以台阁重臣为代表的台阁体诗篇，表面雍容华贵，内里点缀升平；诗词走到成化至正德年间，台阁体有了变化，其中多了些关注社会生活的内容但仍流于虚泛；此后为嘉靖、隆庆年间，大多数诗人看到台阁体的虚浮华丽内容空洞，转而师法古人，此时的诗词创作少了盛唐风采，更多承袭魏晋之风；及至万历、天启年间，一批有识之士起而反对复古模拟倾向，提倡诗歌应"出于己之所得，而不窃于人之所尝言者也"，更加提倡直抒胸臆的"性灵"之说，中国诗词在古人的荫蔽下终于有了耳目一新的创作突破；沿着这条创新之路到达崇祯年间，世相纷乱，正如人们常说的"愤怒出诗人"，这时的中国诗词终于重新充满了战斗性和对现实的观照，然而，遗憾的是，诗词的复兴只经历了短暂荣光便伴随着明朝衰亡而重归寂寞。

　　明成祖永乐十九年，即公元1421年正月，明朝政府正式迁都北京。在明朝浩如烟海的诗词和众多有卓越建树的诗词大家中，刘基和于谦与北京的渊源最深也最为人们所熟悉。

　　杰出的军事谋略家、政治家、文学家和思想家刘基一直被北京人亲切地称为刘伯温，刘伯温建造北京城的故事和童谣至今仍是北京童蒙故事之一。"刘伯温，造北京，造了一座哪吒城。里九外七皇城四，前门楼子在正中。"这首已被收入《北京好歌》之中的童谣，让很多人认为，明朝开国重臣刘基真的参与了缔造北京城，但事实上这并非史实。历史上的刘基与北京并无关系，他卒于1375年，其时距离明成祖迁都北京尚有46年之遥。

　　刘基是活在北京人心中、口中的一代天骄，尽管传说跨越了时间、地域而被赋予传奇色彩，但抛开这些，仅从其在明朝文坛的地位论，他是当之无愧的诗词大家。他与宋濂、高启并称"明初诗文三大家"。日本学者奥野纯评价他："际会风云，平定海宇，既辟一代之规模，又阐一代之文章，盖诚意伯刘公一人而已矣。"类似出于近现代大儒、学者的对刘基的赞誉非常之多。现代文学研究者评价刘基的诗歌，"具有沉郁凝重、雄放奇崛、古朴雅健三种不同的艺术风格，这些又都是为表现他忧世之叹和忧生之嗟服务，是内容与形式的完美结合。其词在内容上大致可分为哀民生之多艰，叹壮志之难酬，愤言之不听和借景抒情、咏物寓意之作。风格特点上表现为内容长于托物寄兴、行文长于铺叙、摹景状物秀丽入神"。刘基之所以深得百姓敬仰，与他的忧国忠君、关注民生有着密切关系，他一生诗作中这样的作品不胜枚举。如在《次韵和谦上人秋兴七首（一）》中有句："一自中原万马奔，江淮今有几州存？"在《雨雪曲》中，他面对千村萧瑟、万户悲歌的荒凉景象发问："黎民亦何辜，骨肉散草莱？"在《田家》中感叹道："租税所从来，官府宜爱惜。"

刘基一生留下各类文章220多篇、诗1301首、词211阕。他的诗词以一个政治家的敏锐目光和博大胸怀，继承和发挥了杜甫的现实主义优秀诗风，具有鲜明的时代气息和深广的社会内容。《明史》说他："所为文章，气昌以奇，与宋濂并为一代之宗。"清著名评论家沈德潜在《明诗别裁集》评价他的诗词"独标高格"，"超然独胜，允为一代之冠"。清《四库全书》总目提要评论："其诗沉郁顿挫，自成一家，足与高启相抗。"

在明朝的诗坛，真正无论个人命运还是政治生涯都与北京紧密相连的诗人非于谦莫属。就像熟悉"人生自古谁无死，留取丹心照汗青"一样，北京人深深记得这首《石灰吟》："千锤万凿出深山，烈火焚烧若等闲。粉骨碎身全不怕，要留清白在人间。"这首诗是曾主持了历史上著名的北京保卫战的英雄将领于谦的代表作。

于谦（1398—1457年），一生为官廉洁正直，曾平反冤狱，救灾赈荒，深受百姓爱戴。明英宗时，瓦剌入侵，英宗被俘。于谦议立景帝，亲自率兵固守北京，击退瓦剌。这便是在北京建都史上反复被提及的北京保卫战。北京保卫战的胜利，体现了于谦作为一代名将、一代名臣的军事才华和保家卫国的民族大义。于谦率领的明军仅在五天时间内迅速击败敌军，不仅加强了京师部队的战斗力，组成了一支战斗力较强的机动兵力，使瓦剌军不敢窥视京师，而且还促进了边防建设，收复了许多要塞和重镇，使明王朝的统治得到了进一步的加强。

对于明王朝和北京来说，北京保卫战的胜利是一大幸事，但对于谦来说，恰恰是这场注定要名垂青史的战役，使他的身后格外悲凉。被瓦剌放回的明英宗在宦官和佞臣的拥戴下发动夺门之变，于景泰八年（1457年）正月重登帝位，废景帝为成王。而当年拥立景帝并力主抗敌的于谦却在石亨、徐有贞等卑劣政客的诬蔑下被英宗杀害。于谦被害令天下人扼腕。一名叫陈逵的官员悄悄收殓了他的遗骸，于谦的女婿把灵柩运回故乡杭州，与南宋抗金名将岳飞一样葬在西子湖畔。也正因此，后人用"赖有岳于双少保（注：岳飞、于谦二人均曾被加封少保），人间始觉重西湖"的诗句来缅怀两位民族英雄的气节和千秋功绩。

刘基和于谦，一虚一实，是中国诗坛的骄傲，也是北京和北京人的骄傲。

清 人生如初见便山山水水成十万诗篇

一六一六至一九一一

在经历了明朝后期的诗词复兴和复归淡静之后，清朝，中国的诗词再一次发展到蔚为壮观的"盛世"。清朝的诗词中不乏反映社会矛盾和现实社会生活的作品，在技巧形式上也不断追求创新，为诗歌的发展积累了艺术经验。清代诗人善于借鉴前代，扬长补短，兼学唐宋诗的长处，流派纷呈，风格多样，其成就超过元明两代，足以下启近代。

清朝是诗人辈出的时代。清初有顾炎武、王夫之、黄宗羲、钱谦益、吴伟业等著名学者诗人；清中叶有沈德潜、郑板桥、张问陶、袁枚、蒋士铨、赵翼等艺术家诗人；晚清则有龚自珍、魏源、黄遵宪以及康有为、梁启超、谭嗣同等思想家、革命家诗人……其洋洋大观，数不胜数。

历史长河中明珠难于尽数，但清代在诗词创作上有独到建树并留下"奇葩"的两位北京本土诗词圣手，当数乾隆皇帝和满族贵族出身的纳兰性德。

在中国文学史中，乾隆皇帝没有以诗人身份名列其中，但如果从作诗和留下诗作的数量上来说，他当得起"中国第一诗人"，他的43000余

清高宗爱新觉罗·弘历（1711-1799年），清朝第六位皇帝，定都北京后第四位皇帝，年号乾隆，寓意"天道昌隆"。他25岁登基，在位60年，退位后当了3年太上皇，实际掌握最高权力长达63年4个月，是中国历史上执政时间最长、年寿最高的皇帝。

首御制诗，几乎直追唐朝290年间遗下的近5万首唐诗的数量总和。清代大学士梁诗正曾经赞美乾隆"圣天子好古勤求"。乾隆自幼受儒家礼教文化熏陶，四书五经、诗词歌赋、书法绘画无一不精，学识渊博、治国有方，在清朝的皇帝中其历史地位仅次于他爷爷康熙皇帝。因为他喜欢到处题诗，所谓"乾隆遗风"广为人知。

作为"诗歌爱好者"的乾隆皇帝在北京留下了无数"诗迹"，不必说颐和园、紫禁城等这些皇家胜迹，就连偶然经过的小村庄，他也会因诗兴大发而留下"墨宝"。然而，或许也是因为他贵为天子的身份和总喜欢语出惊人的个性，他的数万首诗中真正被传诵者少之又少。乾隆的诗中喜欢用一些鲜为人知的词语，造成了诗句的艰涩难懂，又或者因为酷爱诗词，他总是习惯性地拘泥于格律而使大多诗作成为平仄对仗的堆砌文字。基于此，后人常以为他爱炫耀知识，而忽略了乾隆御制诗中真正的佳作。

在中国诗词发展史上，有婉约词、豪放词等等分类，名称不一而足，但清朝有一位作词的大家，以其名字流传，自成一格，他就是"纳兰词"的主人纳兰性德。

纳兰性德出身于贵族家庭，其父亲是康熙时期的"相国"明珠，母亲爱新觉罗氏为英亲王阿济格第五女、一品诰命夫人。而其家族那拉氏隶属正黄旗，为清初满族最显赫的八大姓之一，即后世所称的"叶赫那拉氏"。纳兰性德自幼天资聪颖，读书过目不忘，17岁入国子监读书，19岁起主持编纂了一部1792卷的儒学汇编——《通志堂经解》，此后修史、著书，表现出相当广博的学识和意趣。康熙十三年（1674年），与妻子卢氏结婚，两年后卢氏因难产去世，纳兰的悼亡之音破空而起，成为他的代表词集《饮水词》中的高峰。近代著名学者王国维曾给其极高赞扬："纳兰容若以自然之眼观物，以自然之舌言情。此由初入中原未染汉人风气，故能真切如此。北宋以来，一人而已。"而晚清词人况周颐也在《蕙风词话》中誉其为"国初第一词手"。

至今，年轻人常会在情关流离处发出"人生若只如初见"的感慨，又有多少人知道这一名句出自纳兰性德之手？"人生若只如初见，何事秋风悲画扇？等闲变却故人心，却道故人心易变。"这首《木兰花令·拟古决绝词》便是这流转到今日的名句的出处。而能写下如此通透诗句的纳兰性德，也是一名随时随处流露真性情的本真之人。22岁时，康熙皇帝授他三等侍卫官职，很快升为一等。他以英俊威武的武官身份参与风流斯文的诗文之事，随皇帝南巡北狩，游历四方，是人们羡慕的文武兼备的年少英才，帝王器重的随身近臣，前途无量的达官显贵。但作为诗文艺术的奇才，他在内心深处厌倦官场庸俗和侍从生活，无心功名利禄，"身在高门广厦，常有山泽鱼鸟之思"。24岁时，他把自己的词作编选成集，名为《侧帽集》，又著《饮水词》，再后有人将两部词集增遗补缺，共349首，编辑一处，合为《纳兰词》。传世的《纳兰词》在当时社会上就享有盛誉，为文人、学士等高度评价，成为那个时代词坛的杰出代表。

纳兰性德还是一位真心促进文化发展的名仕。他广交天下有识之士，仗义疏财，他的住所渌水亭（现北京宋庆龄故居内恩波亭）一度因文人骚客雅聚而著名，这些人切磋文化、畅谈天下文章，促进了康乾盛世的文化繁荣。

遗憾的是，纳兰性德英年早逝，一代词人卒于1685年，时年仅31岁。民国时期北京小说家张恨水先生的《春明外史》中写到一位才子，死于30岁的壮年，其友恸道："看到平日写的词，我就料他跟那纳兰容若一样，不能永年的……"可见纳兰性德和纳兰词的影响之深远已经渗透到后世文学、文化的各个方面。纳兰性德的诗词中，有不少是因扈驾游历北京西山一带风景名胜时写作的。这些地方至今几乎都有迹可循，有史可稽，成为北京历史上与山河齐名的瑰宝。

德国古典诗人荷尔德林有过一句流传甚远的诗句："人，诗意地栖居。"同样来自德国的哲学家海德格尔曾用这样的句子对其进行解释："如果我们把这多重之间称作世界，那么世界就是人居住的家……"

对于北京人而言，有860余年建都史、有远远超过860余年诗词发展史的北京，是一个可以诗意地栖居的诗意的精神家园，富丽堂皇，珍宝遍布，当之无愧。

章节·柒

霓裳 嘉韵天成

如果没记错,那是1983年的北京颐和园。4月初,玉兰盛开。她被她母亲牵着手,一直牵到玉兰树下。但是她不想就这样素淡着留下一张和大多数与玉兰合影者面貌相近的照片,不远处,"旗装"拍照的小亭子吸引了她。她跑着过去,想问问穿上旗装拍照要多少钱,然而跑近了,她很失望,原来那"旗装"不能移动,只是惟妙惟肖的一具纸板,人站在纸板后面,把头伸进"衣领"与"头饰"之间,便可以拍出好似真穿了慈禧太后年轻时那身红色旗袍的感觉……

时间到了1989年,还是北京颐和园,还是4月初玉兰盛开时,在相同的地点,她终于遇见"真正的"旗装。虽然因为本身是旅游纪念照的"道具",水红色袍子已经破旧,头饰上的大牡丹也略显衰败,但这不能挡住她的热情,她要和她的"旗袍梦"中的锦绣美衣相拥着留下纪念。于是,就有了在24年后怎么看怎么觉得青涩的一段旧时光浮在一张老照片上。

和她一样的北京女子,大多有过自己的服饰之梦,而这个梦,与有着860余年都城史的北京所历经的金、元、明、清四朝服饰有千丝万缕的联系。当中国电影明星穿着青花瓷花样的礼服或者金丝彩绣的"龙袍"走在法国戛纳的红地毯上,当来到中国学说相声、学唱京剧的外国人穿上一件中式唐装以示对华夏文化的仰慕,在世界的喝彩和外来者的喟叹之中,她,或者她的北京同伴,从箱子底或者衣柜深处拎出来一件带着樟脑味的华服——真正的绫罗绸缎或者绢帛素麻,掐了牙子带着镶滚钉着手工盘扣珠片绣花的那么一件满含了古典贵族气值得一辈子收藏的北京瑞蚨祥手做唐装,哗啦地一抖,谁能说落在地上的不是860余年来北京的一部服饰史?

镶珠绣金山林熊虎皆入画成衫
一一一五至一二三四

即便是能征惯战的马上民族，爱美之心也不会因此打折扣。金代的女真人虽然留下的可供考据的服饰文物不多，却凭着《大金国志》和《金史·舆服志》中的相关记载让后人惊讶于他们在衣着方面的讲究。

金代的服饰文物遗存少而又少，与他们实行火葬有关。在北京、辽宁、内蒙古、黑龙江等地出土的屈指可数的金代墓葬都有火焚印迹，致使遗存的服饰实物更加少见。在金太祖完颜阿骨打建立金朝之前，女真人附属于辽，有金以来，女真人向着燕地进发，他们发现辽国的发达也体现在注重服饰礼仪制度，于是依样学样，有了南北官制。接着，他们挺近黄河流域，又发现了宋代冠服制度的优雅完备，于是继续吸纳学习，有了自己的皇帝冕服、通天冠、绛纱袍，自此无限细分，皇太子有远游冠，百官朝服、冠服越来越复杂，达到基本与宋制一样繁琐，甚至颜色也有了详尽的规定，比如公服五品以上用紫色、六品和七品则是绯色、八品和九品只能着绿色，款式为盘领横纴袍，为了与卫士区别开，文官还要佩戴金银鱼袋。

随着海陵王入主金中都，金朝官员的制服越来越华丽，官服的胸部、肩袖上用金绣做装饰。金世宗时更发明了按官职尊卑定绣花大小的方式，三品以上绣五寸花，六品以上三寸，官职越低花朵越小，到了小吏则全无绣花，只能穿芝麻罗。金人虽然一手缔造了金中都，一举成为"北京人"，他们也深受汉服的影响，吸收了很多汉族人的服饰文化，但是，他们从没忘记自己出身于白山黑水之间，原本是骁勇的马背民族。这一点，在金代衣服的花纹内容和款式上即可看出。金朝官服按穿用季节有详细分类，通常春水之服绣鹘捕鹅，中间配合以花卉，秋山之服则大多以熊鹿山林为内容。官服的款式为窄袖、盘领，且腋下不缝合，前后襟连接处作褶裥，衣长只到小腿胫骨间，这一切都是为了便于骑马。为官的总是要比平民富裕，衣服绣金还不够，腰带上还要镶嵌宝物。这也是按照为官的级别来确定，腰带镶玉为上等，金次之，犀角象骨又次之。腰带上还可以挂牌子、刀子和其他杂用品。

至于衣服的材质，金人与后世的最大不同在于他们喜欢穿"裘皮"。《大金国志》中有记载："化外不毛之地，非皮不可御寒，所以无贫富皆服之。富人春夏多以紵丝、锦䌷为衫裳，亦间用细皮、布。秋冬以貂鼠、狐貉或羔皮，或作紵丝绸绢。贫者春秋并衣衫裳，秋冬亦衣牛、马、猪、羊、猫、犬、熊、蛇之皮，或獐、鹿、麇皮为衫。裤、袜皆以皮。"大概这也是他们不"忘本"的表现之一吧。

一个王朝的繁荣与否，常常体现在女人的衣饰之上。金朝女性有一种叫做襜裙的下衣极有特色，《金史·舆服志》中曾有女真女子喜穿遍绣全枝花的黑紫色六裥襜裙的记载，这个襜裙据《大金国志》描写，是把细细的铁丝围成圈架再挂上里衬，这样外面的裙子裙摆自然蓬起，想象其样貌应该颇似现代礼服中的所谓"蓬蓬裙"。这样一位金国女子穿上团衫，腰间系上红红绿绿的腰带，该是如何窈窕可人。更不用说还有根据其丈夫的尊贵程度"配发"给她们的云肩、霞帔用以强调她们的贵族身份。

在北京辽金城垣博物馆，可以看到金代服装的展示。很多人看过之后表示有"似曾相识"之感，比如直领交叠、左衽和束带，比如那种为了劳动方便、骑射便捷而留下的开衩和防止绊住自己而特意设计的短小尺码……与汉族服装以及此后蒙古人带入的蒙古族服饰交相融合，汇为一条难分彼此的服饰长河。

元 不缕金堆绣无侍儿搀扶怎说奢华

一二七一至一三六八

元朝的大都处处体现着多元文化的杂糅和并蓄，农耕文化、草原文化加上欧洲的基督教文化、西亚的伊斯兰文化造就了元代服饰的多样。

最初，蒙古族沿袭着他们一贯"披发椎髻、冬戴帽、夏戴笠"的服饰穿用方式，用貂鼠、羊皮制成的皮帽、皮袄、皮靴是他们最为平常的装束。作为中国历史上的少数民族政权之一，元朝建立之后，全国按照种族分为蒙古人、色目人、汉人、南人四等，众多朝廷命官由蒙古贵族充任，色目人担当各种副职。这种在社会地位上的区分，也体现在服饰上。通常，蒙古贵族衣着华丽，色目人次之，汉人、南人大多衣着朴素。

早在蒙古族入关之前，汉族服饰文化历史已历经数个朝代的变迁、发展并自成一体，影响深远，吸引着各族人民的目光并广为学习，蒙古族也不例外。元朝早期，便引进了汉族的朝祭服饰，将官员的服装分为冕服、朝服、公服等。在遗存的元代壁画和绘画作品中，常常能看到元朝官吏穿着大袖、盘领、右衽的长袍。元朝官员以佩牌体现等级森严，第一等贵臣佩虎斗金牌，次为素金牌，再次为银牌。看腰间佩牌的材质，即可明了此人的身份地位。

曾经，元朝被称作"大汗之国"，大都被认为是"黄金之城"。乾元肇始，政治稳定、经济快速发展，纺织工业从惨遭战乱破坏到重新振兴，其分工也越来越精细，无论丝织业还是刺绣工艺，都达到了极高水准。国家富庶，则服饰鲜艳、材质精良、细节

考究。因此，元代的服装大多讲究"加金"，缕金织物大行其道，所谓"纱、罗、绞、縠，无不加金"，大都之内王公贵族行止之处每每金光闪闪。据史料记载，当时元人最热衷的衣料叫作"纳石失"，也就是波斯金锦。在这里不能不提到《马可·波罗行纪》，尽管关于他是否真的曾经在元大都生活过，学界至今有不同的声音，但是，他对元大都社会生活的描述却有相当一部分符合《元史》以及各种文存的记载。据马可·波罗在他的游记中所写，在元代统治者每年举行的13次大朝会上，有爵位的达官贵族参加者约12000人，帝王、大臣在大殿前用金杯按爵位、亲疏、辈分祝酒，高官的服装即多用彩色织金锦，上面绣着的花朵大小尺寸标志着其人的品级高低。最吸引人的无疑是皇帝身上的珠玉装饰、缕金堆绣，格外华美。同时，他描写皇帝出行狩猎时坐于内用金锦、貂皮、银鼠皮装饰，外用豹皮覆盖的大木楼内，由四只大象抬着木楼前进，其"金灿灿"无人能比。

元朝从皇帝到文武百官将"质孙衣"作为内庭大宴的服饰，其分类和各种饰物的搭配方式非常繁琐。按节令，质孙衣有冬夏之分，分别各有十数种；按照穿用的季节和场合又有不同的搭配，穿金锦衬剪茸的质孙衣，要戴金锦暖帽等，讲究衣冠配套。元代皇室贵族的帽子上大多镶有宝石，除了来自各处的贡献，也有开疆拓土、征服欧亚过程中不可避免的劫掠。红宝石、蓝宝石、猫儿眼、祖母绿等彩色宝石从此成为珍宝，价格一路飙升至今。传说忽必烈在万寿日穿的是金光耀眼华丽无比的长袍，同时赐给2000名贵族和武官同样颜色和款式的礼服，上面装饰着宝石和珍珠，用今天的话说真是挥金如土的大手笔。

在当下可见的描摹元代女性生活起居和日常情态的绘画等艺术品中，依稀可见当时贵族女性的骄奢模样。有趣的是，那些体态丰腴的女子大多有侍女搀扶且长衣及地，有的还戴着从头顶向上延伸两三尺的长冠。有学者考证，这种长冠名叫罟罟冠（也称顾姑冠、姑姑冠），戴着的女子忌讳别人触摸，出入庐帐时必须侧身低头。考究的贵族女子将这顶长冠装饰得极为华美，冠顶扩大成平顶帽的形状，用红绢、金锦、青毡等包裹，镶上翠花、珍珠，地位更高的人还会在冠顶插野鸡毛，轻移脚步时野鸡毛飞动起来，格外有型。与长冠相配的是长袍。蒙古贵族妇女的袍子宽松肥大，袖身很大但袖口收窄，最亮眼的是，此长袍真正符合这个"长"字，"藏身"长袍的女子每每会为其曳地的长度所累，靠自己行走几无可能，因此走路时要有至少两名女奴搀扶才能前行。有关中国历代服饰变迁的史料中介绍，这种长身宽袍通常用织金锦、丝绒或毛织品制成，使用胭脂红、鸡冠紫、泥金等饱和度高的"大色"。入主京城的蒙古族贵妇，早已一改马上民族的彪悍，而将汉族人的婀娜窈窕作为审美标准，这也体现了蒙汉服饰文化的融合以及汉族服饰文化为蒙古族服饰带来的新变化。

明 布衣皇帝制服饰等级难掩别有洞天

一三六八至一六四四

明朝的开国皇帝洪武帝朱元璋是布衣出身，据说，他在戎马生涯开始之前有过多年"过苦日子"的经历，民间流传着他挨饿、乞讨、当和尚混饭吃的故事，版本众多。他的妻子后来的马皇后也是克勤克俭、荆钗布裙的劳动妇女。待到这样一对男女成了一国之君和"第一贵妇"，他们容不得为了奇装异服、比财斗富而铺张浪费。元朝人衣饰之上金光灿烂的那一套，他们从一开始就极为反感，必须制止。

洪武元年（1368年），明太祖朱元璋甫一立国，即下令禁"胡服"，恢复汉人衣冠，"悉命复衣冠如唐制"，而后，更加详尽地对全国官民百姓衣冠服饰的形制、质地和颜色作出严格规定。这些规定翻译成今天的文字需要很长的说明，细致到士民怎样束发、官员的乌纱帽怎样戴、衣服的领子必须是圆领、靴子则必须是黑靴等等。接着，进一步按照身份和行当对百姓和女子加以规定："士庶则服四带巾、杂色盘领衣，不得用黄、玄；乐工冠青字顶巾，系红绿帛带；士庶妻首饰许用银镀金，耳环用金珠，钏镯用银，服浅色，团衫用丝、绫罗、绸绢；其乐妓则戴明角冠，皂褙子，不许与庶民妻同。"

大家都按照规定的款式和颜色来穿还不够，两年之后，朱元璋又对衣料和首饰作出了细致规定。不管是男人还是女人，衣着要朴素，"不得用金绣锦绮丝绫罗，止用绸绢素纱，首饰、钏镯不得用金玉珠翠,止用银,靴不得裁制花样、金钱装饰"。如此,仍意犹未尽,三年后,对民间女子的衣着颜色有了明确规定,民妇的礼服只能用紫色,一般生活装用色必须浅淡,元朝贵妇喜欢的诸如大红、黄色等夺人眼球的"大色"一概不得使用。

  作为对把钱花在衣服上深恶痛绝的布衣皇帝,朱元璋算是跟大明朝人的穿戴较上了劲,并且行使皇帝的权力,实现"立法"。洪武十三年(1380年)颁布的《大明律》中有"服舍违式"条款,如果有人胆敢不严格遵照自己的身份和地位谨慎着装,做出"越级"穿用服饰的行为,则依法"各问以应得之罪",有官职的人杖责一百、罢免官职,普通老百姓鞭笞五十、连坐家长。不仅如此,饶是挨了打、丢了官,不该穿不该用的那些服饰用品还要没收充公。

明太祖朱元璋一生传奇，可谓皇帝中的奇人奇才，经他一手操作推行的明代服饰制度细致、完整，空前绝后，也奠定了明朝服饰的高贵、端庄、清秀、简素的儒雅风格。在大批明代壁画和绘画艺术品中，清癯、俊逸的儒生与名仕比比皆是，温婉、贤淑的女子别有韵致。

明朝的服饰制度不可谓不严苛，但即便如此，中国服饰文化发展到明朝中后期还是达到了一个新的高点。随着社会经济的发展，带动了人们对服饰个性化的追求，明中期以降，整个社会的服饰风格从朴素趋于艳丽，气度华美，成为近世中国服饰艺术的典范。

就像明太祖朱元璋亲力亲为完成的明朝服饰制度格外繁缛一般，明朝服饰中从冠带到鞋履再到大大小小的饰品难以尽述，然而有几样别具特色的"发明创造"不能不提。

首先是"瓜皮帽"。明初，穿着青布直身的宽大长衣，头上戴状如半个西瓜、以六瓣、八瓣布片缝合的小帽，这样的男人最为多见，可算得上是当时的"时尚达人"。因为方便好戴、气质纯朴，这种帽子很快流行起来，这便是后来清代颇成气候的"瓜皮小帽"的前身。

另一样开天辟地的物件便是明朝官服上的补子。补子的历史可以追溯到唐武则天时,到了元朝,有一种"胸背",即在服装的前胸后背部装饰动物纹样,到了明朝,"胸背"被创造性发挥成为补子,装饰在官员常服的前胸后背处,并以图案的不同表示官阶的高低,这种补子一直沿用到清朝。当然,擅长制定服饰制度的朱元璋对补子也没有"姑息",在《明会典》中,补子的图案被作了严格规范,比如:只有公侯驸马才可以在补子上绣麒麟;文官的补子上要绣禽类,表示文明;武官则绣兽类,显示威猛;文官武官各分为九品,每一品级的补子上绣什么动物又有具体规定。至今,人们在古装影视剧和戏剧舞台上仍然可以看到各式各样的补子,只是这些补子上绣什么,已经无须顾忌朱元璋的意见。

对于促进中国服饰文化的发展,明朝妇女功不可没。明朝妇女喜欢合身、窄瘦、修长的衣服,而这时的上下衣与元朝以及金朝女性衣服的长度比例完全不同,金元妇女衣裙大多上短下长,明朝女性衣裙则变为长衣、长裙。有学者这样描述明朝妇女的裙子:"裙幅初为六幅,这是遵循古仪,即所谓'裙拖六幅湘江水';到了明代末年,裙幅始用八幅,腰间细褶数十,行动辄如水纹。到了明末,裙子的装饰日益讲究,裙幅也增至十幅,腰间的褶裥越来越密,每褶都有一种颜色,轻描淡绘,色极清雅,微风吹来,色如月华,故称'月华裙'。此外,还有用绸缎剪成大小规则的条子,每条绣以花鸟图纹,另在两边镶以金线,称凤尾裙;又有一种,以整缎折以细道,称为百褶裙。"令人惊喜的是,这段文字中描述的这些裙子的款式,不仅流传到清朝、到民国、到近现代,即便是当下,也仍然没有淡出时尚舞台。

清 一口钟罩不住精致华美艳惊后世

一六一六至一九一一

关于服饰的故事讲到清朝，旗袍则必须出场。有多少人念念不忘电影《花样年华》中的几十款花色各异的旗袍被张曼玉穿得风情万种，然而，此旗袍非彼旗袍，流行于民国之后的中式旗袍并非清王朝建立时满族男女的旗袍。为了将这两种不同的旗袍区分开来，姑且将后者叫作旗装吧。

随着清王朝建立并定都北京，满族和汉族的服饰文化便开始融合。史料记载，顺治九年（1652年），钦定《服色肩舆条例》颁行，从此废除了浓厚汉民族色彩的冠冕衣裳。明代男子一律蓄发挽髻，着宽松衣，穿长统袜、浅面鞋；清时则剃发留辫，辫垂脑后，穿瘦削的马蹄袖箭衣、紧袜、深统靴。

与金代女真人和元朝蒙古人一样，清军未曾入关时，满族人游牧征战于关外，紧身、简洁、方便骑射成为旗装的最大特点，与宽袍大袖的汉族服装形成了鲜明的对比。清朝统治者对自

身的民族服装格外珍爱，不仅将旗装当作祖先的传统加以继承，更重要的是，他们认为旗装轻便简洁的特点决定了他们能从马背上得天下，屡战屡胜，因此，他们对继承、保护和发展民族服饰极为重视，于是，清朝的服饰也成为中国历代服饰中最繁缛、复杂者，同时也凭着独特的魅力影响至今。

有人这样描述旗装："旗装外轮廓呈长方形，马鞍形领掩颊护面，衣服上下不取腰身，衫不露外，偏襟右衽以盘纽为饰，假袖二至三幅，马蹄袖盖手，镶滚工艺装饰，衣外加衣，增加坎肩或马褂……其造型完整严谨，呈封闭式盒状体，因此形象肃穆庄重，清高不凡，而独树一帜，突破了几千年来飘逸的塔形衣冠，给世人留下深刻的形象记忆。"

清朝也是中国与其他国家交往最为频繁的朝代，西风东渐和东风西渐形成了东西方文化各个领域的融合与并蓄。清朝的服饰不仅融合了金元少数民族服饰文化的精华，也吸收了明朝以及明朝所承袭的汉服文化中的精粹，加上满族自身的服饰礼制，形成了新型的中国风范。无论从清朝帝王官员的冕服、冠服、公服到民间士人百姓的常规服饰，都有详细的穿用制度和礼仪规范，其复杂考究集历朝之大成。及至当代，人们耳熟能详的那些包含了唐装元素的"龙袍""蟒袍""旗袍"以及舞台、T台上的华服，都可以看到清代服饰的影子。

清朝服饰的款式、材质、制作工艺、穿用规范极尽繁缛奢华，细节越发精致考究，举不胜举。清朝的官服中继续沿用了明朝的补子，但在以图案表明官阶品级的规制上又有了许多改变，其使用的精绣纹样有了更具象化的规定。与明朝相比，清代女性的服饰变化最大。清代仕女服饰内容则主要以旗装为主，包括旗袍、大衫、大褂、宽口裤、宽褶裙等等。这类服饰大多为合领、右衽，领、襟、袖使用宽大的边作为修饰，袖子短而口宽，长及手；袍在身侧开高衩，下穿宽口大裤，足穿花盆鞋。明朝女性喜爱的长衫长裙仍然是服饰的主流之一，在旗装之外，爱美的清朝女性以大褂和大衫为外衣，"合领右衽，短袖而宽"；下穿宽大的百褶裙，裙长及足，内穿宽口大裤。值得一提的是，清代妇女有一种名为"一口钟"的斗篷，这是一种无袖、不开衩的长披风，有抽口领、高领和低领之分，用鲜艳的绸缎面料绣以颜色丰富的纹饰，有些在领口镶滚皮毛边作为装饰，通常里子也用温暖柔软的裘皮，冬季穿戴将人自颈项以下全部遮住，既能御寒又能于行动中体现体态的柔美。清代礼仪复杂，穿"一口钟"的女子在行礼前必须将其脱去，否则被认为是不合礼数、不讲礼貌。与"一口钟"相辉映的则是女人喜爱的云肩。云肩在金代及更早的汉唐服饰中已有，是妇女披在肩上的饰品。最初，清代女子将云肩用在婚礼上，而后，江南女子的发髻大多低垂，担心弄脏了衣领，于是以云肩作为"遮挡"，这种起源于日常生活中的小物逐渐发展到被贵族妇女用作

装饰，有剪彩做莲花形、结丝线成为璎珞，或以珍珠串联并辅以其他贵重珠玉，形成"肩头的时尚"和身份与财富的象征。或许，当代女子喜爱的各式各样、各种材质、色彩斑斓、面料精美的披肩也与云肩有着内在联系。

清朝服饰的制作工艺达到了当时的极高水准，那时的中国"时尚人士"设计制作的各类服饰令人惊艳。在北京故宫博物院，藏有一张意大利画家郎世宁绘制的清朝乾隆皇帝在南苑阅兵的《大阅铠甲骑马像》，画中皇帝的铠甲

十分精彩。清朝的铠甲分甲衣和围裳并配以盔帽，其中以大阅甲为最精美。大阅甲不是用金属做成，而是用金线在黄缎上绣出金版纹，代替甲上的金属叶。胄即盔帽，"用牛皮制，髹以漆，嵌以东珠，并饰有金梵文。甲衣的护领、护肩、护腋、前胸后背、前挡、袖端上都绣有串珠绣的龙纹和彩云、寿山福海纹。下面的两幅围裳各饰行龙戏珠，以金版纹间隔，行裳侧边及底边饰升龙和行龙。护心镜亦以云龙纹板围护。"

这幅画作中的乾隆皇帝富丽威严，栩栩如生。

清朝的服饰遗存在中国历史上历朝历代的服饰文物中为最多，也对近现代及当代的服饰文化和北京地区的民间服饰风格产生了深远影响。

从1153年海陵王完颜亮率部跨越白山黑水入主金中都，直到中国最后一个封建王朝清朝在历史的烟云里渐行渐远，直至今日，北京860余年的都城史和着860余年间中国人服饰的演变，步调一致、互为佐证，见证着这座城市的文明进程。时尚是历史的边角，而拉动其每一个细节，都可以看到一代代中国人追求美好生活的梦想，从未改变，从未停歇。

后记

逢北京建都860年之际，有机会满怀敬意和骄傲地为这座城市梳理她辉煌灿烂、博大精深的历史文化中的一鳞半爪，有机会满怀敬畏和自豪地为这座城市写下这些其实并不足以状写其精彩之万一的文字，是北京赋予我们的机遇和使命。

感谢为北京缔造千秋功业的古圣前辈和今天的同伴，感谢860余年来穷毕生之力为北京修书的先贤大儒和当代学者，感谢为今天的北京打造中国特色世界城市无私奉献的城市建设者。因为你们，北京将继续辉煌；与你们携手，我们共同见证！

生而有幸，我们在北京。

参考文献

侯仁之著：《北京城的生命印记》，中国出版集团三联书店，2009年9月版

《辽史》（全五册），中华书局点校本，2011年5月版

《金史》（全八册），中华书局点校本，2011年3月版

《元史》（全十五册），中华书局，1976年版

孟森著：《孟森明史讲义》，中华书局，2009年5月版

万斯同编著：《明史》(全八册)，上海古籍出版社，2008年1月版

吴晗著：《明朝三百年》，国际文化出版公司，2011年10月版

[美] 牟复礼、[英] 崔瑞德编著，张书生等译：《剑桥中国明代史（1368—1644年）》（上、下卷），中国社会科学出版社，1992年2月版

[意] 马可波罗著，沙海昂注释，冯承钧译：《马可波罗行纪》，商务印书馆，2012年6月版

爱新觉罗·溥仪著：《我的前半生》，群众出版社，2013年1月版

[英] 庄士敦（Reginald Flemjng Johnston）著，秦传安译：《紫禁城的黄昏》，中央编译出版社，2010年4月版

徐振清、贾云江主编：《辽金史论集》第九辑（金史国际学术研讨会专集），中州古籍出版社，1996年版

鲍海春、王禹浪主编：《金史研究论丛》（第二届金史国际学术研讨会论文专辑），哈尔滨出版社，2000年版

阎凤梧主编：《全辽金文》（全三册），山西古籍出版社，1999年版

阎凤梧、康金声主编：《全辽金诗》（全三册），山西古籍出版社，2002年版

中国社会科学院历史研究所宋辽金元史研究室编：《宋辽金史论丛》（第一辑），中华书局，1985年版

中国社会科学院历史研究所宋辽金元史研究室编：《宋辽金史论丛》（第二辑），中华书局，1991年版

周峰著：《完颜亮评传》，民族出版社，2002年版

刘肃勇著：《金世宗传》，三秦出版社，1986年版

范军、周峰著：《金章宗传》，中国广播电视出版社，2003年版

周惠泉著：《金代文学论》，东北师范大学出版社，1997年版

李正民、董国炎主编：《辽金元文学研究》，文化艺术出版社，1999年版

于杰、于光度著：《金中都》，北京出版社，1989年版

郝树侯、杨国勇著：《元好问传》，山西人民出版社，1990年版

[宋] 宇文懋昭撰，崔文印校证：《大金国志校证》（全二册），中华书局，1986年版

[宋] 叶隆礼撰，贾敬颜、林荣贵校：《契丹国志》，上海古籍出版社，1985年版

徐慕云著：《中国戏剧史》，上海古籍出版社，2001年2月版

王国维著：《宋元戏曲史》，中华书局，2010年8月版

[日] 田仲一成著，布和译，吴真注译：《中国戏剧史》，北京大学出版社，2011年7月版

黄能馥、乔巧玲著：《衣冠天下：中国服装图史》，中华书局，2009年11月版

沈从文著：《中国古代服饰研究》，上海书店出版社，2011年7月版

孟森著：《清史讲义》，中华书局，2010年1月版

郑天挺著：《清史》，天津人民出版社，2011年5月版

王钟翰著：《清史十六讲》，中华书局，2009年1月版

王钟翰注释：《清史列传》，中华书局，1987年11月版

赵敏俐著：《中国诗歌史通论》，人民文学出版社，2013年3月版

朱和平、郭孟良著：《中国书画史会要》，中州古籍出版社，2009年12月版

曹宝麟著：《中国书法史：宋辽金卷》，江苏教育出版社，2009年4月版

黄惇著：《中国书法史：元明卷》，江苏教育出版社，2009年4月版

刘恒著：《中国书法史：清代卷》，江苏教育出版社，2009年4月版

同时参考北京大学、中国人民大学、复旦大学、中山大学、郑州大学、南开大学、北京师范大学等高校相关学术论文，此处不一一列举，一并致谢

图书在版编目（CIP）数据

北京城纪/安顿主编. -- 北京：五洲传播出版社,2017.3
ISBN 978-7-5085-2774-1

Ⅰ.①北… Ⅱ.①安… Ⅲ.①城市史 - 研究 - 北京 Ⅳ.①K291

中国版本图书馆CIP数据核字(2017)第037874号

北京城纪

主　　编：	王　琳
执行主编：	安　顿
撰　　稿：	安　顿
责任编辑：	宋博雅
编　　辑：	曲　静　王　勇
图片编辑：	桑　浥　马　柯
装帧设计：	杨小军　生　晨　吕良华
出版发行：	五洲传播出版社
地　　址：	北京市海淀区北三环中路31号生产力大楼B座6层
邮　　编：	100088
电　　话：	010-82005927，010-82007837（发行部）
网　　址：	http://www.cicc.org.cn　http://www.thatsbooks.com
印　　刷：	廊坊市恒泰印务有限公司
版　　次：	2017年4月第1版第1次印刷
开　　本：	787mm×1092mm　1/16
印　　张：	8
字　　数：	130千字
定　　价：	46.00元